Martin McDonagh
Plays: 1

The Beauty Queen of Leenane, A Skull in Connemara, The Lonesome West

The Leenane Trilogy: 'Confirms McDonagh as both a writer of staying power and an individual talent within a powerful tradition, with something distinctive and important to say. His is a voice you will want to hear again.' *Sunday Times*

The Beauty Queen of Leenane: 'His ear for the absurdities of speech, his control of a potentially fatal undercurrent of violence, the mordantly black humour which turns your laughter into horror in a split-second, add up to a pungent, poignant drama.' *Mail on Sunday*

A Skull in Connemara: 'The play is part whodunnit, part blood-soaked comedy-farce, a combination of brutish violence and raw, rowdy, black comedy.' *Sunday Times*

The Lonesome West: 'An extraordinary play where two brothers, one of whom has killed their father, are closeted together in undying hostility like a penned-up Cain and Abel.' *Guardian*

Martin McDonagh's first play *The Beauty Queen of Leenane* was the 1996 winner of the George Devine Award, won the Writer's Guild Award for Best Fringe Play and also the Evening Standard Award for Most Promising Newcomer. The play was nominated for six Tony awards, of which it won four, and a Lawrence Olivier award (the BBC Award for Best New Play). *The Beauty Queen of Leenane* is the first in Martin McDonagh's *Leenane Trilogy*; *A Skull in Connemara* and *The Lonesome West* complete the cycle. *A Skull in Connemara* was nominated for an Oliver Award for Best New Comedy. Martin McDonagh's most recent play, *The Cripple of Inishmaan*, is the first in a new trilogy of Aran Island plays.

by the same author

The Cripple of Inishmaan
The Lieutenant of Inishmore

MARTIN MCDONAGH

Plays: 1

The Leenane Trilogy

The Beauty Queen of Leenane

A Skull in Connemara

The Lonesome West

introduced by Fintan O'Toole

Methuen Drama

METHUEN DRAMA CONTEMPORARY DRAMATISTS

9 10 8

This collection first published in Great Britain in 1999
by Methuen Publishing Limited

Methuen Drama
A & C Black Publishers Ltd
36 Soho Square
London W1D 3QY

www.methuendrama.com

The Beauty Queen of Leenane first published in Great Britain in 1996,
by Methuen Drama Ltd
Copyright © 1996 by Martin McDonagh
A Skull in Connemara first published in Great Britain in 1997,
by Methuen Drama Ltd
Copyright © 1997 by Martin McDonagh
The Lonesome West first published in Great Britain in 1997,
by Methuen Drama Ltd
Copyright © 1997 by Martin McDonagh
This collection copyright © 1999 by Martin McDonagh
Introduction copyright © 1999 by Fintan O'Toole

The right of Martin McDonagh to be identified as the author of this
work has been asserted by him in accordance with the Copyright,
Designs and Patents Act, 1988

ISBN 978 0 413 71350 6

A CIP catalogue record for this book
is available from the British Library

Typeset by Deltatype Ltd, Birkenhead, Merseyside

Printed and bound in Great Britain by
CPI Cox & Wyman, Reading, Berkshire

Contents

Martin McDonagh
A Chronology

1996   *The Beauty Queen of Leenane* opens the new Town
        Hall Theatre, Galway in a Druid Theatre
        Company/Royal Court co-production and later
        transfers to the Royal Court Theatre Upstairs,
        London. Winner of the George Devine Award,
        the Writers' Guild Award for Best Fringe Play
        and the Evening Standard Award for Most
        Promising Newcomer. The play is nominated for
        a Lawrence Olivier Award (the BBC Award for
        Best New Play).

1997   *The Cripple of Inishmaan*, winner of the 1996/7
        Pearson Television Theatre Writers' Scheme Best
        Play prize and the first in a new trilogy of Aran
        Island plays, opens at the Royal National
        Theatre, London.
        A Skull in Connemara and *The Lonesome West*
        première in Ireland and London in a Druid/
        Royal Court co-production. Presented with a
        second revival of *The Beauty Queen of Leenane*, the
        three plays form *The Leenane Trilogy*. *A Skull in
        Connemara* is nominated for a Lawrence Olivier
        Award for Best New Comedy.

1998   *The Beauty Queen of Leenane* opens at the Atlantic
        Theater in New York and then transfers to
        Broadway in April. The play is nominated for six
        Tony awards, including Best Play, and is the
        winner of four.
        The Cripple of Inishmaan opens in a new production
        at the Joseph Papp Public Theater in New York.

1999   The US première of *The Lonesome West* due to
        open on Broadway.
        The Beauty Queen of Leenane still playing on
        Broadway.

Introduction

For the Irish exile in England, home thoughts from abroad are supposed to carry a familiar resonance. Over a century ago, W.B. Yeats popularised the mode in 'The Lake Isle of Inishfree' when he stood in London 'on the roadway or on the pavements grey' and heard 'lake water lapping with low sounds by the shore' of an idyllic island in West of Ireland. Later, the commercial songwriters and folk balladeers churned out songs about exiles writing to the sweethearts they left behind where the Mountains of Mourne sweep down to the sea or promising to take the sweethearts they brought with them home again, Cathleen. The melancholy allure of a lost paradise, where the sweet sorrow of parting will one day be transformed into the joy of homecoming, hung over everything, making London a bleak nowhere and Ireland a primaeval fantasy.

Martin McDonagh, the son of a Sligo mother and a Galway father, grew up in this kind of London. He had Irish aunts and uncles all around. His family lived on a block in Elephant and Castle where half the houses were occupied by Irish families. It was a similar story when they moved down the road to Camberwell. He spent his summer holidays in Easkey, County Sligo and in Connemara, the western region of County Galway. He became a choir boy in the Catholic parish church and grew up steeped in the emotive stories of Irish nationalism. Later, his parents moved back to Lettermullan in Connemara, and although he and his older brother stayed behind in London, they continued to spend their summers in Ireland. He was, and is, a citizen of an indefinite land that is neither Ireland nor England, but that shares borders with both.

He is, too, part of a generation that has completely redefined the term 'Anglo-Irish'. It used to mean, in Brendan Behan's scabrous definition, 'a Protestant on a horse', a member of the old Irish ascendency with deep cultural and political affinities for England. Much of twentieth-century Irish theatre – Yeats, John Synge, Augusta Gregory, Denis Johnston – is rooted, however uncomfortably, in that tradition. Now, though, Anglo-Irish has come to mean a new kind of fusion that arises, not from ascendency but from exile. The children of Irish emigrants, growing up with all the accents and attitudes of urban England are finding or making their own connections with Irish culture. In music, the songwriter and singer Shane McGowan is the obvious example. In sport, it is Jack Charlton's Irish soccer team of the late 1980s and early 1990s. In the theatre now it is Martin McDonagh.

For him, there was none of the exile's longing, none of the proper nostalgic clutch of the ould sod. There was no 'Irish community', just people who happened to be around the place. The childhood influences of Catholicism and nationalism wore off. And yet, there was, for him, a crucial Ireland. It was not a place or a faith or a community or even a family. It was not even, as you might expect from a young writer, a literary or theatrical culture: Synge or Yeats, Joyce or Beckett, though Synge's *The Playboy of the Western World* is certainly a presence behind *A Skull in Connemara* and the same play's title is from a line in Beckett's *Waiting for Godot*. It was just a voice in the head, a way of talking.

Wanting to develop a style of dialogue as strange and heightened as those of David Mamet or Harold Pinter but yet free of their obvious influence, he returned to the rhythms and structures, the twists and elisions of Irish speech. Not, of course, that his dialogue is a mere faithful transcription of everyday Irish conversation, any more than Synge really heard the great poetry of *The Playboy* by listening to the peasants' talk through a crack in the floorboards. In it, Harold Pinter and Joe Orton blend seamlessly with Tom Murphy and John B. Keane to create a vibrantly original mixture of absurd comedy

and cruel melodrama. McDonagh's London-Irish
background allows him to hold in perfect tension an
extraordinary range of elements from both sides of the
Irish Sea.

As in Pinter, everyday banality acquires sinister
undertones. As in Orton, mundane speech is bent into
outrageous shapes without ever losing its demotic feel.
But there is also a dark comedy of yearning and despair
reminiscent of Murphy, and, in *The Beauty Queen of
Leenane*, a situation − a forty-year-old spinster trapped
with a monstrous old woman in a remote house in the
West − that echoes his great play *Bailegangaire*. There is a
wildly melodramatic plot of which the early John B.
Keane might have been proud. And all of this is held
together with an utterly 1990s sensibility, in which
knowing and playful pastiche becomes indistinguishable
from serious and sober intent.

The mixture of elements makes sense because the
country in which McDonagh's play is set is pre-modern
and post-modern at the same time. The 1950s is laid
over the 1990s, giving the play's apparent realism the
ghostly, dizzying feel of a superimposed photograph. All
the elements that make up the picture are real, but their
combined effect is one that questions the very idea of
reality.

One of the superimposed pictures is a black-and-white
still from an Abbey play of the 1950s: west of Ireland
virgins and London building sites, tyrannical mothers
and returned Yanks, family feuds, clerical crises of faith.
But the other picture is a lurid Polaroid of a postmodern
landscape, a disintegrating place somewhere between
London and Boston, saturated in Irish rain and
Australian soaps, a place in which it is hard to
remember anyone's name, in which news of murders
floats in through the television screen, in which the
blurring of personal identities makes the line between
the real and the unreal dangerously thin. And behind
these garish colours, there are shadows in which

madness and violence lurk, waiting to emerge. Looking at both pictures at the same time, you experience a series of double takes. You are drawn into the comfortable, melodramatic rush of the plot, knowing all the time that it is taking you places you don't want to go, wondering why conversations keep throwing up images of violence and death, trying to remember if these people are coming from a funeral or a party.

And as the real and the unreal become increasingly hard to tell apart, the whole idea of theatrical realism becomes itself the biggest double-take of all. The conversations of domestic drama are at once followed and parodied. The domestic details – Kimberley biscuits, lumpy Complan, Tayto crisps, sausage rolls – that ought to provide a 'realistic' backdrop to the action are instead pushed relentlessly into the foreground by McDonagh's brilliant dialogue. And the domestic appliances that seem to signal the conventions of familiar naturalism become gradually less cosy and more sinister, as objects like cookers, cooking oil and pokers become portents of violence and cruelty. In *A Skull in Connemara*, even the kitchen table has skulls and skeletons on it.

It is easy to be fooled by the apparently traditional, naturalistic form of the plays. On the surface, they seem to hark back to the kitchen sink Irish realism of the 1950s and to refer to an archaic world of frustrated spinsters, lonely bachelors and spoiled priests. But it is well to remember that, in *The Beauty Queen of Leenane*, the kitchen sink is the focus for an especially grotesque and pungent running joke. McDonagh's Leenane is, at one level, still stuck in the 1930s. But that frozen, locked-in society has moved forty years forward in time. It exists now at the fringes of a high tech, post-modern Ireland shaped by media imagery, by multinational companies, and by tourism.

Behind these images, there is a profound and convoluted sense of displacement. Pato Dooley in *The Beauty Queen of Leenane* sums it up when he confesses to

Maureen that although he is unhappy in London, he
does not dream of returning forever to Leenane: 'when
it's there I am, it's here I wish I was, of course. Who
wouldn't? But when it's here I am ... it isn't *there* I
want to be, of course not. But I know it isn't here I
want to be either.' These people are neither here nor
there. They don't know whether they're coming or
going. The old exile's nostalgia has been replaced by a
less tangible but more unsettling sense of loss.

Part of this loss is the inability to pine for the idyllic
landscape that surrounds them. Nature as a source of
beauty, consolation or inspiration is almost entirely
absent from their lives. Nature is the rain and the mud
and the steep rocky hills that you have to drag yourself
up. It is the decaying flesh and bare bones of the dead
in the local graveyard. The lake that ought to be
awesome is the 'cold and bleak' place in which lonely
men drown themselves. The animal kingdom, for all the
notice they take of it, seems to be reduced to rustled
cows, chickens killed with tennis balls, dogs with their
ears shorn, and baked hamsters. Pato in *The Beauty Queen*
does remember 'the mountains and the green' of
Leenane, but only when he's away from them.

Pictures and images of the landscape have replaced
the thing itself. Ray Dooley in *The Beauty Queen* asks
'Who wants to see Ireland on telly?' but the place is
crawling with tourists who come looking for where *The
Quiet Man* was made. The most poignant expression of
longing for home comes when Maureen in the same
play recalls her time in Leeds, cleaning offices and
toilets. A woman from Trinidad shows her pictures of
home, and Maureen responds by showing her a
'calendar with a picture of Connemara on'. A calendar
picture of Connemara evokes a warmth that Connemara
itself cannot. For, in spite of the outward appearances of
rustic simplicity, this is a media-soaked world.

Before these plays, no one had quite managed to
describe the mental universe of people who live on the

margins of a globalized culture. McDonagh's West of Ireland is, at one level, even more remote and lonely than Synge's. But, in an age of electronic communications and mass marketing, it is also saturated with objects and media images that float in like alien spacecraft. The landscape is littered with Swingball sets and Kimberley biscuits, Spiderman and stagecoaches, werewolf comics and Ker-Plunk, Complan and *Hill Street Blues*. Manufactured images – plaster saints, Australian soaps, American cop shows, songs on the radio – arouse as much emotion and obsession as real people do. The trappings of the plays themselves, the sets and props and the machinery of the plots, are, in a sense, another kind of received image. They are displaced remnants of a culture that has died.

For almost everything that gave that old Ireland its sense of itself is gone. The Church is falling apart. Religion is a spent force, and its remnants reside in weird vestiges like Valene's figurines of saints and Virgins or the vol-au-vents that are served after funerals. The priest, Father Welsh, reckons that 'God has no jurisdiction in this town. No jurisdiction at all.' He knows that 'I'm a terrible priest and I run a terrible parish.' The Catholic faith has melted like Valene's plastic saints and martyrs when his brother, out of spite, bakes them in the brand-new stove.

The State that generations of nationalists fought to establish is represented in *A Skull in Connemara* by the ineffectual, melancholy policeman Thomas Hanlon, so intent on his fantasies of being an American TV cop that he can't see the murders that are going on around him or notice the blood on Mick Dowd's clothes. Far from halting the violence or the self-destruction of the community, he joins in both.

Irish history itself is an evanescent emotion or a lurid joke. Mick in *A Skull in Connemara* makes a spectacularly sick joke about the most sacred of Irish historical memories, the Great Famine of the 1840s. Maureen in

The Beauty Queen of Leenane flashes with momentary indignation at 'the English stealing our language and our land'. But England is where many of the people in the plays end up, and the Irish language is just a vague memory.

Connemara, where the plays are set, is supposed to be a Gaeltacht, an official preserve of native Gaelic speech. But in McDonagh's language, Gaelic is just a pale ghost behind the vernacular English of the characters, its dead forms clinging on to an empty afterlife in the baroque syntax of their speech. Where a Gaelic word like 'gasur' (boy) intrudes on the dialogue, it serves only to remind us of an absent, half-forgotten tongue.

The sacred memory of the dead is no longer honoured. *A Skull in Connemara* centres on the literal digging up of the bones of the ancestors. The dead cannot rest in peace, but must be yanked from the ground to make room for the new corpses that are queuing up to occupy it. When characters in the plays – Mags, Thomas, Father Welsh – die, there is no feeling that the community is bereft. After the vol-au-vents, there will be amnesia.

And the greatest Irish institution of all – the family – hardly seems in great shape either. Mother and daughter are locked in a struggle to the death. A husband may have killed his wife. A son has blown the head off his father. Two sets of brothers – the Hanlons and the Connors – are at each other's throats. The possibility of a happy marriage for Maureen and Pato is a hope raised only to be dashed. Even sex doesn't seem particularly likely. Valene, Coleman, Welsh and Maureen are probably virgins. When Maureen and Pato get to bed, they don't manage to consummate their desires.

As descriptions of sociological reality, these are, of course, dramatic exaggerations. But they are not pure inventions. McDonagh makes sure that the action is continually brushing up against verifiable actuality.

Contemporary events do sneak their way into the plays, so that every time the audience sinks into the comfortable feeling of lapsing into a world that has long passed, it is jolted with a reminder that all of this is very much of the 1990s. Ray Dooley in *The Beauty Queen* ludicrously compares his own experience of breaking his toes while trying to kick down the door of a police cell to the plight of the Birmingham Six, Irishmen jailed in Britain for terrorist crimes they did not commit. The violent conflict in Northern Ireland, and in particular an atrocity in Belfast in the early 1990s when Loyalist paramilitaries murdered five Catholics in a bookie's shop, is referred to in *A Skull in Connemara* when Mick Dowd undercuts Thomas Hanlon's fantasy of being a detective in *Hill Street Blues*: 'Go ahead up north so. You'll be well away. Hang about a bookies or somewhere.'

The vicious civil wars that followed the breakup of Yugoslavia in the early 1990s are made to impinge momentarily on *The Lonesome West* when Valene, reading a women's magazine, notices 'a lad here in Bosnia and not only has he no arms but his mammy's just died.' And the scandals that beset the Irish Catholic church in the 1990s echo briefly through the plays. When Mag in *The Beauty Queen* tells Ray that 'There was a priest in the news Wednesday had a babby with a Yank!', the reference to the Bishop of Galway (the diocese in which the real Leenane is situated), Eamonn Casey, who did just that, is unmistakable. Equally, when Coleman in *The Lonesome West* comforts Father Welsh by telling him that, however inadequate he may be, at least he doesn't abuse children, the humour is all the blacker and all the funnier because it touches the painful reality of the child abuse scandals that rocked the Irish church in the mid- and late 1990s.

These reminders of the real world serve to stave off nostalgia, to place the action in the proper time-frame, and to create an unsettling, almost surreal fusion of fable

and reportage. But they also draw attention to the
universality of violence. By bringing the slaughter of
Bosnia and Northern Ireland or the failings of British
justice to mind they destroy any illusion that the bloody
death and petty cruelty that afflict this fictional Leenane
are either wild exaggerations or peculiar, endemic Irish
failings. The savagery of the plays may not be literal but
neither is it pure invention. It comes from a vividly
imagined sense of cultural confusion, from a world in
which meanings and values have been shattered into
odd-shaped fragments. And what's important is that the
plays themselves try to put those fragments back together
again. McDonagh weaves an extraordinary range of
images into the assured stagecraft of the well-made play.
There are touches of Shakespeare and soap opera,
Grand Guignol and the Bible, melodrama and the
Brothers Grimm. Dirty realism is continually shading
into heightened epic. The graveyard scenes of *A Skull in
Connemara* hang somewhere between a cheap vampire
movie and the fourth act of Hamlet. Valene and
Coleman in *The Lonesome West* remind us at one moment
of Bobby and J.R. in *Dallas*, at another of Cain and
Abel in the Book of Genesis. Mag in *The Beauty Queen of
Leenane* is at once a figure from an old Irish country
melodrama and the wicked stepmother from Snow
White.

And what matters in the end is that McDonagh is
more than just a very clever theatrical stylist. His tricks
and turns have a purpose. They are bridges over a deep
pit of sympathy and sorrow, illuminated by a tragic
vision of stunted and frustrated lives. Moments of love
and loss, of yearning and even of faith catch the light
now and then. That they cannot abide long in such a
blighted world seems somehow less remarkable than the
fact that they arise at all.

Fintan O'Toole

The Beauty Queen of Leenane

The Beauty Queen Of Leenane, a Druid Theatre Company/Royal Court Theatre co-production, was first presented at the Town Hall Theatre, Galway, on 1st February 1996, marking the official opening of the theatre, and subsequently opened at the Royal Court Theatre Upstairs on 5th March 1996. The cast was as follows:

Mag   Anna Manahan
Maureen   Marie Mullen
Ray   Tom Murphy
Pato   Brian F. O'Byrne

Directed by Garry Hynes
Designed by Francis O'Connor
Lighting designed by Ben Ormerod
Sound by David Murphy

The Druid Theatre Company/Royal Court Theatre production was subsequently produced by Atlantic Theater Company, Randall L. Wreghitt, Chase Mishkin, Steven M. Levy and Leonard Soloway in association with Julian Schlossberg and Norma Langworthy on 14th April 1998.

Characters

Maureen Folan, *aged forty. Plain, slim.*
Mag Folan, *her mother, aged seventy. Stout, frail.*
Pato Dooley, *a good-looking local man, aged about forty.*
Ray Dooley, *his brother, aged twenty.*

Setting: Leenane, a small town in Connemara, County Galway.

Scene One

*The living-room/kitchen of a rural cottage in the west of Ireland. Front
door stage left, a long black range along the back wall with a box of turf
beside it and a rocking-chair on its right. On the kitchen side of the set is a
door in the back wall leading off to an unseen hallway, and a newer oven,
a sink and some cupboards curving around the right wall. There is a
window with an inner ledge above the sink in the right wall looking out
onto fields, a dinner table with two chairs just right of centre, a small TV
down left, an electric kettle and a radio on one of the kitchen cupboards, a
crucifix and a framed picture of John and Robert Kennedy on the wall
above the range, a heavy black poker beside the range, and a touristy-
looking embroidered tea-towel hanging further along the back wall,
bearing the inscription 'May you be half an hour in Heaven afore the
Devil knows you're dead'. As the play begins it is raining quite heavily.*
Mag Folan, *a stoutish woman in her early seventies with short, tightly
permed grey hair and a mouth that gapes slightly, is sitting in the
rocking-chair, staring off into space. Her left hand is somewhat more
shrivelled and red than her right. The front door opens and her daughter,*
Maureen, *a plain, slim woman of about forty, enters carrying
shopping and goes through to the kitchen.*

Mag Wet, Maureen?

Maureen Of course wet.

Mag Oh-h.

Maureen *takes her coat off, sighing, and starts putting the shopping
away.*

Mag I did take me Complan.

Maureen So you *can* get it yourself so.

Mag I can. (*Pause.*) Although lumpy it was, Maureen.

Maureen Well, can I help lumpy?

Mag No.

Maureen Write to the Complan people so, if it's lumpy.

Mag (*pause*) You do make me Complan nice and smooth.
(*Pause.*) Not a lump at all, nor the comrade of a lump.

Maureen   You don't give it a good enough stir is what you don't do.

Mag   I gave it a good enough stir and there was still lumps.

Maureen   You probably pour the water in too fast so. What it says on the box, you're supposed to ease it in.

Mag   Mm.

Maureen   That's where you do go wrong. Have another go tonight for yourself and you'll see.

Mag   Mm. (*Pause.*) And the hot water too I do be scared of. Scared I may scould meself.

Maureen *gives her a slight look.*

Mag   I *do* be scared, Maureen. I be scared what if me hand shook and I was to pour it over me hand. And with you at Mary Pender's, then where would I be?

Maureen   You're just a hypochondriac is what you are.

Mag   I'd be lying on the floor and I'm not a hypochondriac.

Maureen   You are too and everybody knows that you are. Full well.

Mag   Don't I have a urine infection if I'm such a hypochondriac?

Maureen   I can't see how a urine infection prevents you pouring a mug of Complan or tidying up the house a bit when I'm away. It wouldn't kill you.

Mag (*pause*)   Me bad back.

Maureen   Your bad back.

Mag   And me bad hand. (**Mag** *holds up her shrivelled hand for a second.*)

Maureen (*quietly*)   Feck . . . (*Irritated.*) I'll get your Complan so if it's such a big job! From now and 'til doomsday! The one thing I ask you to do. Do you see Annette or Margo coming pouring your Complan or buying your oul cod in butter sauce for the week?

Mag No.

Maureen No is right, you don't. And carrying it up that hill. And still I'm not appreciated.

Mag You *are* appreciated, Maureen.

Maureen I'm not appreciated.

Mag I'll give me Complan another go so, and give it a good stir for meself.

Maureen Ah, forget your Complan. I'm expected to do everything else, I suppose that one on top of it won't hurt. Just a . . . just a blessed fecking skivvy is all I'm thought of!

Mag You're not, Maureen.

Maureen *slams a couple of cupboard doors after finishing with the shopping and sits at the table, after dragging its chair back loudly. Pause.*

Mag Me porridge, Maureen, I haven't had, will you be getting? No, in a minute, Maureen, have a rest for yourself . . .

But **Maureen** *has already jumped up, stomped angrily back to the kitchen and started preparing the porridge as noisily as she can. Pause.*

Mag Will we have the radio on for ourselves?

Maureen *bangs an angry finger at the radio's 'on' switch. It takes a couple of swipes before it comes on loudly, through static – a nasally male voice singing in Gaelic. Pause.*

Mag The dedication Annette and Margo sent we still haven't heard. I wonder what's keeping it?

Maureen If they sent a dedication at all. They only said they did. (**Maureen** *sniffs the sink a little, then turns to* **Mag**.) Is there a smell off this sink now, I'm wondering.

Mag (*defensively*) No.

Maureen I hope there's not, now.

Mag No smell at all is there, Maureen. I do promise, now.

Maureen *returns to the porridge. Pause.*

Mag   Is the radio a biteen loud there, Maureen?

Maureen   A biteen loud, is it?

Maureen *swipes angrily at the radio again, turning it off. Pause.*

Mag   Nothing on it, anyways. An oul fella singing nonsense.

Maureen   Isn't it you wanted it set for that oul station?

Mag   Only for Ceilidh Time and for whatyoucall.

Maureen   It's too late to go complaining now.

Mag   Not for nonsense did I want it set.

Maureen (*pause*)   It isn't nonsense anyways. Isn't it Irish?

Mag   It sounds like nonsense to me. Why can't they just speak English like everybody?

Maureen   Why should they speak English?

Mag   To know what they're saying.

Maureen   What country are you living in?

Mag   Eh?

Maureen   What country are you living in?

Mag   Galway.

Maureen   Not what county!

Mag   Oh-h . . .

Maureen   Ireland you're living in!

Mag   *Ireland.*

Maureen   So why should you be speaking English in Ireland?

Mag   I don't know why.

Maureen   It's Irish you should be speaking in Ireland.

Mag   It is.

Maureen   Eh?

Mag   Eh?

Maureen   'Speaking English in Ireland.'

Mag (*pause*)   Except where would Irish get you going for a job in England? Nowhere.

Maureen   Well, isn't that the crux of the matter?

Mag   Is it, Maureen?

Maureen   If it wasn't for the English stealing our language, and our land, and our God-knows-what, wouldn't it be we wouldn't need to go over there begging for jobs and for handouts?

Mag   I suppose that's the crux of the matter.

Maureen   It *is* the crux of the matter.

Mag (*pause*)   Except America, too.

Maureen   What except America too?

Mag   If it was to America you had to go begging for handouts, it isn't Irish would be any good to you. It would be English!

Maureen   Isn't that the same crux of the same matter?

Mag   I don't know if it is or it isn't.

Maureen   Bringing up kids to think all they'll ever be good for is begging handouts from the English and the Yanks. That's the selfsame crux.

Mag   I suppose.

Maureen   Of course you suppose, because it's true.

Mag (*pause*)   If I had to go begging for handouts anywhere, I'd rather beg for them in America than in England, because in America it does be more sunny anyways. (*Pause.*) Or is that just something they say, that the weather is more sunny, Maureen? Or is that a lie, now?

Maureen *slops the porridge out and hands it to* **Mag**, *speaking as she does so.*

Maureen   You're oul and you're stupid and you don't know what you're talking about. Now shut up and eat your oul porridge.

Maureen *goes back to wash the pan in the sink.* **Mag** *glances at the porridge, then turns back to her.*

Mag   Me mug of tea you forgot!

Maureen *clutches the edges of the sink and lowers her head, exasperated, then quietly, with visible self-control, fills the kettle to make her mother's tea. Pause.* **Mag** *speaks while slowly eating.*

Mag   Did you meet anybody on your travels, Maureen? (*No response.*) Ah no, not on a day like today. (*Pause.*) Although you don't say hello to people is your trouble, Maureen. (*Pause.*) Although some people it would be better not to say hello to. The fella up and murdered the poor oul woman in Dublin and he didn't even know her. The news that story was on, did you hear of it? (*Pause.*) Strangled, and didn't even know her. That's a fella it would be better not to talk to. That's a fella it would be better to avoid outright.

Maureen *brings* **Mag** *her tea, then sits at the table.*

Maureen   Sure, that sounds exactly the type of fella I would *like* to meet, and then bring him home to meet you, if he likes murdering oul women.

Mag   That's not a nice thing to say, Maureen.

Maureen   Is it not, now?

Mag (*pause*)   Sure why would he be coming all this way out from Dublin? He'd just be going out of his way.

Maureen   For the pleasure of me company he'd come. Killing you, it'd just be a bonus for him.

Mag   Killing *you* I bet he first would be.

Maureen   I could live with that so long as I was sure he'd be clobbering you soon after. If he clobbered you with a big axe or something and took your oul head off and spat in your neck, I wouldn't mind at all, going first. Oh no, I'd enjoy it, I would.

No more oul Complan to get, and no more oul porridge to get, and no more . . .

Mag (*interrupting, holding her tea out*)   No sugar in this, Maureen, you forgot, go and get me some.

Maureen *stares at her a moment, then takes the tea, brings it to the sink and pours it away, goes back to* **Mag**, *grabs her half-eaten porridge, returns to the kitchen, scrapes it out into the bin, leaves the bowl in the sink and exits into the hallway, giving* **Mag** *a dirty look on the way and closing the door behind her.* **Mag** *stares grumpily out into space. Blackout.*

Scene Two

Mag *is sitting at the table, staring at her reflection in a hand-mirror. She pats her hair a couple of times. The TV is on, showing an old episode of* The Sullivans. *There is a knock at the front door, which startles her slightly.*

Mag   Who . . . ? Maureen. Oh-h. The door, Maureen.

Mag *gets up and shuffles towards the kitchen window. There is another knock. She shuffles back to the door.*

Who's at the door?

Ray (*off*)   It's Ray Dooley, Mrs. From over the way.

Mag   Dooley?

Ray   Ray Dooley, aye. You know me.

Mag   Are you one of the Dooleys so?

Ray   I am. I'm Ray.

Mag   Oh-h.

Ray (*pause. Irritated*)   Well, will you let me in or am I going to talk to the door?

Mag   She's feeding the chickens. (*Pause.*) Have you gone?

Ray (*angrily*)   Open the oul door, Mrs! Haven't I walked a mile out of me way just to get here?

Mag   Have you?

Ray   I have. 'Have you?' she says.

Mag *unlatches the door with some difficulty and* **Ray Dooley**, *a lad of about nineteen, enters.*

Ray   Thank you! An hour I thought you'd be keeping me waiting.

Mag   Oh, it's you, so it is.

Ray   Of course it's me. Who else?

Mag   You're the Dooley with the uncle.

Ray   It's only a million times you've seen me the past twenty year. Aye, I'm the Dooley with the uncle, and it's me uncle the message is.

Ray *stops and watches the TV a moment.*

Mag   Maureen's at the chickens.

Ray   You've said Maureen's at the chickens. What's on the telly?

Mag   I was waiting for the news.

Ray   You'll have a long wait.

Mag   I was combing me hair.

Ray   I think it's *The Sullivans*.

Mag   I don't know what it is.

Ray   You do get a good reception.

Mag   A middling reception.

Ray   Everything's Australian nowadays.

Mag   I don't know if it is or it isn't.

Mag *sits in the rocking-chair.*

At the chickens, Maureen is.

Ray   That's three times now you've told me Maureen's at the chickens. Are you going for the world's record in saying 'Maureen's at the chickens'?

Mag (*pause. Confused*)   She's feeding them.

Ray *stares at her a moment, then sighs and looks out through the kitchen window.*

Ray   Well, I'm not wading through all that skitter just to tell her. I've done enough wading. Coming up that oul hill.

Mag   It's a big oul hill.

Ray   It *is* a big oul hill.

Mag   Steep.

Ray   Steep is right and if not steep then muddy.

Mag   Muddy and rocky.

Ray   Muddy and rocky is right. Uh-huh. How do ye two manage up it every day?

Mag   We do drive.

Ray   Of course. (*Pause.*) That's what I want to do is drive. I'll have to be getting driving lessons. And a car. (*Pause.*) Not a good one, like. A second-hand one, y'know?

Mag   A used one.

Ray   A used one, aye.

Mag   Off somebody.

Ray   Oul Father Welsh – Walsh – has a car he's selling, but I'd look a poof buying a car off a priest.

Mag   I don't like Father Walsh – Welsh – at all.

Ray   He punched Mairtin Hanlon in the head once, and for no reason.

Mag   God love us!

Ray   Aye. Although, now, that was out of character for Father Welsh. Father Welsh seldom uses violence, same as most young priests. It's usually only the older priests go punching you in the head. I don't know why. I suppose it's the way they were brought up.

Mag   There was a priest the news Wednesday had a babby with a Yank!

Ray   That's no news at all. That's everyday. It'd be hard to find a priest who hasn't had a babby with a Yank. If he'd punched that babby in the head, that'd be news. Aye. Anyways. Aye. What was I saying? Oh aye, so if I give you the message, Mrs, you'll be passing it on to Maureen, so you will, or will I be writing it down for you?

Mag   I'll be passing it on.

Ray   Good-oh. Me brother Pato said to invite yous to our uncle's going-away do. The Riordan's hall out in Carraroe.

Mag   Is your brother back so?

Ray   He is.

Mag   Back from England?

Ray   Back from England, aye. England's where he was, so that's where he would be back from. Our Yankee uncle's going home to Boston after his holiday and taking those two ugly duckling daughters back with him and that Dolores whatyoucall, Healey or Hooley, so there'll be a little to-do in the Riordan's as a goodbye or a *big* to-do knowing them show-off bastards and free food anyways, so me brother says ye're welcome to come or Maureen anyways, he knows you don't like getting out much. Isn't it you has the bad hip?

Mag   No.

Ray   Oh. Who is it has the bad hip so?

Mag   I don't know. I do have the urine infection.

Ray   Maybe that's what I was thinking of. And thanks for telling me.

Mag   Me urine.

Ray   I know, your urine.

Mag   And me bad back. And me burned hand.

Ray   Aye, aye, aye. Anyways, you'll be passing the message on to that one.

Mag   Eh?

Ray   You'll be remembering the message to pass it on to that one?

Mag   Aye.

Ray   Say it back to me so.

Mag   Say it back to you?

Ray   Aye.

Mag (*long pause*)   About me hip . . . ?

Ray (*angrily*)   I should've fecking written it down in the first fecking place, I fecking knew! And save all this fecking time!

Ray *grabs a pen and a piece of paper, sits at the table and writes the message out.*

Talking with a loon!

Mag (*pause*)   Do me a mug of tea while you're here, Pato. Em, Ray.

Ray   *Ray* my fecking name is! Pato's me fecking brother!

Mag   I do forget.

Ray   It's like talking to a . . . talking to a . . .

Mag   Brick wall.

Ray   Brick wall is right.

Mag (*pause*)   Or some soup do me.

Ray *finishes writing and gets up.*

Ray   There. Forget about soup. The message is there. Point that one in the direction of it when she returns from beyond. The Riordan's hall out in Carraroe. Seven o'clock tomorrow night. Free food. Okay?

Mag   All right now, Ray. Are you still in the choir nowadays, Ray?

Ray   I am *not* in the choir nowadays. Isn't it ten years since I was in the choir?

Mag   Doesn't time be flying?

Ray   Not since I took an interest in girls have I been in the choir because you do get no girls in choirs, only fat girls and what use are they? No. I go to discos, me.

Mag   Good enough for yourself.

Ray   What am I doing standing around here conversing with you? I have left me message and now I am off.

Mag   Goodbye to you, Ray.

Ray   Goodbye to you, Mrs.

Mag   And pull the door.

Ray   I was going to pull the door anyways . . .

Ray pulls the front door shut behind him as he exits.

(*Off.*) I don't need your advice!

As **Ray**'*s footsteps fade,* **Mag** *gets up, reads the message on the table, goes to the kitchen window and glances out, then finds a box of matches, comes back to the table, strikes a match, lights the message, goes to the range with it burning and drops it inside. Sound of footsteps approaching the front door.* **Mag** *shuffles back to her rocking chair and sits in it just as* **Maureen** *enters.*

Mag (*nervously*)   Cold, Maureen?

Maureen   Of course cold.

Mag   Oh-h.

Mag *stares at the TV as if engrossed.* **Maureen** *sniffs the air a little, then sits at the table, staring at* **Mag**.

Maureen   What are you watching?

Mag   I don't know *what* I'm watching. Just waiting for the news I am.

Maureen   Oh aye. (*Pause.*) Nobody rang while I was out, I suppose? Ah no.

Mag   Ah no, Maureen. Nobody did ring.

Maureen   Ah no.

Mag   No. Who would be ringing?

Maureen   No, nobody I suppose. No. (*Pause.*) And nobody visited us either? Ah no.

Mag   Ah no, Maureen. Who would be visiting us?

Maureen   Nobody, I suppose. Ah no.

Mag *glances at* **Maureen** *a second, then back at the TV. Pause.* **Maureen** *gets up, ambles over to the TV, lazily switches it off with the toe of her shoe, ambles back to the kitchen, staring at* **Mag** *as she passes, turns on the kettle, and leans against the cupboards, looking back in* **Mag***'s direction.*

Mag (*nervously*)   Em, apart from wee Ray Dooley who passed.

Maureen (*knowing*)   Oh, did Ray Dooley pass, now?

Mag   He passed, aye, and said hello as he was passing.

Maureen   I thought just now you said there was no visitors.

Mag   There was no visitors, no, apart from Ray Dooley who passed.

Maureen   Oh, aye, aye, aye. Just to say hello he popped his head in.

Mag   Just to say hello and how is all. Aye. A nice wee lad he is.

Maureen   Aye. (*Pause.*) With no news?

Mag   With no news. Sure, what news would a gasur have?

Maureen   None at all, I suppose. Ah, no.

Mag   Ah, no. (*Pause.*) Thinking of getting a car I think he said he was.

Maureen   Oh aye?

Mag   A second-hand one.

Maureen   Uh-huh?

Mag   To drive, y'know?

Maureen   To drive, aye.

Mag   Off Father Welsh – Walsh – Welsh.

Maureen   Welsh.

Mag   Welsh.

Maureen *switches off the kettle, pours a sachet of Complan into a mug and fills it up with water.*

Maureen   I'll do you some of your Complan.

Mag   Have I not had me Complan already, Maureen? I have.

Maureen   Sure, another one won't hurt.

Mag (*wary*)   No, I suppose.

Maureen *tops the drink up with tap water to cool it, stirs it just twice to keep it lumpy, takes the spoon out, hands the drink to* **Mag**, *then leans back against the table to watch her drink it.* **Mag** *looks at it in distaste.*

Mag   A bit lumpy, Maureen.

Maureen   Never mind lumpy, mam. The lumps will do you good. That's the best part of Complan is the lumps. Drink ahead.

Mag   A little spoon, do you have?

Maureen   No, I have no little spoon. There's no little spoons for liars in this house. No little spoons at all. Be drinking ahead.

Mag *takes the smallest of sickly sips.*

Maureen   The whole of it, now!

Mag   I do have a funny tummy, Maureen, and I do have no room.

Maureen   Drink ahead, I said! You had room enough to be spouting your lies about Ray Dooley had no message! Did I not meet him on the road beyond as he was going? The lies of you. The whole of that Complan you'll drink now, and suck the lumps down too, and whatever's left you haven't drank, it is over your head I will be emptying it, and you know well enough I mean it!

Mag *slowly drinks the rest of the sickly brew.*

Maureen Arsing me around, eh? Interfering with my life again? Isn't it enough I've had to be on beck and call for you every day for the past twenty year? Is it one evening out you begrudge me?

Mag Young girls should not be out gallivanting with fellas . . . !

Maureen Young girls! I'm forty years old, for feck's sake! Finish it!

Mag *drinks again.*

Maureen 'Young girls'! That's the best yet. And how did Annette or Margo ever get married if it wasn't first out gallivanting that they were?

Mag I don't know.

Maureen Drink!

Mag I don't like it, Maureen.

Maureen Would you like it better over your head?

Mag *drinks again.*

Maureen I'll tell you, eh? 'Young girls out gallivanting.' I've heard it all now. What have I ever done but *kissed* two men the past forty year?

Mag Two men is plenty!

Maureen Finish!

Mag I've finished!

Mag *holds out the mug.* **Maureen** *washes it.*

Two men is two men too much!

Maureen To you, maybe. To you. Not to me.

Mag Two men too much!

Maureen Do you think I like being stuck up here with you? Eh? Like a dried up oul . . .

Mag Whore!

Maureen *laughs.*

Maureen   'Whore'? (*Pause.*) Do I not *wish*, now? Do I not wish? (*Pause.*) Sometimes I *dream*...

Mag   Of being a ...?

Maureen   Of anything! (*Pause. Quietly.*) Of anything. Other than this.

Mag   Well an odd dream that is!

Maureen   It's not at all. Not at all is it an odd dream. (*Pause.*) And if it is it's not the only odd dream I do have. Do you want to be hearing another one?

Mag   I don't.

Maureen   I have a dream sometimes there of you, dressed all nice and white, in your coffin there, and me all in black looking in on you, and a fella beside me there, comforting me, the smell of aftershave off him, his arm round me waist. And the fella asks me then if I'll be going for a drink with him at his place after.

Mag   And what do you say?

Maureen   I say 'Aye, what's stopping me now?'

Mag   You don't!

Maureen   I do!

Mag   At me funeral?

Maureen   At your bloody wake, sure! Is even sooner!

Mag   Well that's not a nice thing to be dreaming!

Maureen   I know it's not, sure, and it isn't a *dream*-dream at all. It's more of a day-dream. Y'know, something happy to be thinking of when I'm scraping the skitter out of them hens.

Mag   Not at all is that a nice dream. That's a mean dream.

Maureen   I don't know if it is or it isn't.

Pause. **Maureen** *sits at the table with a pack of Kimberley biscuits.*

I suppose now you'll never be dying. You'll be hanging on forever, just to spite me.

Mag   I *will* be hanging on forever!

Maureen   I know well you will!

Mag   Seventy you'll be at my wake, and then how many men'll there be round your waist with their aftershave?

Maureen   None at all, I suppose.

Mag   None at all is right!

Maureen   Oh aye. (*Pause.*) Do you want a Kimberley?

Mag (*pause*)   Have we no shortbread fingers?

Maureen   No, you've ate all the shortbread fingers. Like a pig.

Mag   I'll have a Kimberley so, although I don't like Kimberleys. I don't know why you get Kimberleys at all. Kimberleys are horrible.

Maureen   Me world doesn't revolve around your taste in biscuits.

Maureen *gives* **Mag** *a biscuit.* **Mag** *eats.*

Mag (*pause*)   You'll be going to this do tomorrow so?

Maureen   I will. (*Pause.*) It'll be good to see Pato again anyways. I didn't even know he was home.

Mag   But it's all them oul Yanks'll be there tomorrow.

Maureen   So?

Mag   You said you couldn't stand the Yanks yesterday. The crux of the matter yesterday you said it was.

Maureen   Well, I suppose now, mother, I will have to be changing me mind, but, sure, isn't that a woman's prerogative?

Mag (*quietly*)   It's only prerogatives when it suits you.

Maureen   Don't go using big words you don't understand, now, mam.

Mag (*sneers. Pause*)   This invitation was open to me too, if you'd like to know.

Maureen (*half-laughing*)   Do you think you'll be coming?

Mag   I won't, I suppose.

Maureen   You suppose right enough. Lying the head off you, like the babby of a tinker.

Mag   I was only saying.

Maureen   Well, don't be saying. (*Pause.*) I think we might take a drive into Westport later, if it doesn't rain.

Mag (*brighter*)   Will we take a drive?

Maureen   We could take a little drive for ourselves.

Mag   We could now. It's a while since we did take a nice drive. We could get some shortbread fingers.

Maureen   Later on, I'm saying.

Mag   Later on. Not just now.

Maureen   Not just now. Sure, you've only just had your Complan now.

Mag *gives her a dirty look. Pause.*

Maureen   Aye, Westport. Aye. And I think I might pick up a nice little dress for meself while I'm there. For the do tomorrow, y'know?

Maureen *looks across at* **Mag**, *who looks back at her, irritated. Blackout.*

Scene Three

Night. Set only just illuminated by the orange coals through the bars of the range. Radio has been left on low in the kitchen. Footsteps and voices of **Maureen** *and* **Pato** *are heard outside, both slightly drunk.*

Pato (*off, singing*)   'The Cadillac stood by the house . . . '

Maureen (*off*)   Shh, Pato . . .

Pato (*off. Singing quietly*)   'And the Yanks they were within.' (*Speaking.*) What was it that oul fella used to say, now?

Maureen (*off*)   What oul fella, now?

Maureen *opens the door and the two of them enter, turning the lights on.* **Maureen** *is in a new black dress, cut quite short.* **Pato** *is a good-looking man of about the same age as her.*

Pato   The oul fella who used to chase oul whatyoucall. Oul Bugs Bunny.

Maureen   Would you like a cup of tea, Pato?

Pato   I would.

Maureen *switches the kettle on.*

Maureen   Except keep your voice down, now.

Pato (*quietly*)   I will, I will. (*Pause.*) I can't remember *what* he used to say. The oul fella used to chase Bugs Bunny. It was something, now.

Maureen   Look at this. The radio left on too, the daft oul bitch.

Pato   Sure, what harm? No, leave it on, now. It'll cover up the sounds.

Maureen   What sounds?

Pato   The smooching sounds.

He gently pulls her to him and they kiss a long while, then stop and look at each other. The kettle has boiled. **Maureen** *gently breaks away, smiling, and starts making the tea.*

Maureen   Will you have a biscuit with your tea?

Pato   I will. What biscuits do you have, now?

Maureen   Em, only Kimberleys.

Pato   I'll leave it so, Maureen. I do hate Kimberleys. In fact I think Kimberleys are the most horrible biscuits in the world.

Maureen   The same as that, I hate Kimberleys. I only get them to torment me mother.

Pato   I can't see why the Kimberley people go making them at all. Coleman Connor ate a whole pack of Kimberleys one time and he was sick for a week. (*Pause.*) Or was it Mikados? It was some kind of horrible biscuits.

Maureen   Is it true Coleman cut the ears off Valene's dog and keeps them in his room in a bag?

Pato   He showed me them ears one day.

Maureen   That's awful spiteful, cutting the ears off a dog.

Pato   It *is* awful spiteful.

Maureen   It would be spiteful enough to cut the ears off anybody's dog, let alone your own brother's dog.

Pato   And it had seemed a nice dog.

Maureen   Aye. (*Pause.*) Aye.

Awkward pause. **Pato** *cuddles up behind her.*

Pato   You feel nice to be giving a squeeze to.

Maureen   Do I?

Pato   Very nice.

Maureen *continues making the tea as* **Pato** *holds her. A little embarrassed and awkward, he breaks away from her after a second and idles a few feet away.*

Maureen   Be sitting down for yourself, now, Pato.

Pato   I will. (*Sits at table.*) I do do what I'm told, I do.

Maureen   Oh-ho, do you now? That's the first time tonight I did notice. Them stray oul hands of yours.

Pato   Sure, I have no control over me hands. They have a mind of their own. (*Pause.*) Except I didn't notice you complaining overmuch anyways, me stray oul hands. Not too many complaints at all!

Maureen   I had complaints when they were straying over that Yank girl earlier on in the evening.

Pato   Well, I hadn't noticed you there at that time, Maureen. How was I to know the beauty queen of Leenane was still yet to arrive?

Maureen 'The beauty queen of Leenane.' Get away with ya!

Pato Is true!

Maureen Why so have no more than two words passed between us the past twenty year?

Pato Sure, it's took me all this time to get up the courage.

Maureen (*smiling*) Ah, bollocks to ya!

Pato *smiles.* **Maureen** *brings the tea over and sits down.*

Pato I don't know, Maureen. I don't know.

Maureen Don't know what?

Pato Why I never got around to really speaking to you or asking you out or the like. I don't know. Of course, hopping across to that bastarding oul place every couple of months couldn't've helped.

Maureen England? Aye. Do you not like it there so?

Pato (*pause*) It's money. (*Pause.*) And it's Tuesday I'll be back there again.

Maureen Tuesday? This Tuesday?

Pato Aye. (*Pause.*) It was only to see the Yanks off I was over. To say hello and say goodbye. No time back at all.

Maureen That's Ireland, anyways. There's always someone leaving.

Pato It's always the way.

Maureen Bad, too.

Pato What can you do?

Maureen Stay?

Pato (*pause*) I do ask meself, if there was good work in Leenane, would I stay in Leenane? I mean, there never will be good work, but hypothetically, I'm saying. Or even bad work. Any work. And when I'm over there in London and working in rain and it's more or less cattle I am, and the young fellas cursing over cards and drunk and sick, and the oul digs over there, all pee-stained mattresses and nothing to do but watch the clock . . . when it's there I am, it's here I wish I was, of course. Who wouldn't? But when it's here I am . . . it isn't *there* I want to be, of course not. But I know it isn't here I want to be either.

Maureen   And why, Pato?

Pato   I can't put my finger on why. (*Pause.*) Of course it's beautiful here, a fool can see. The mountains and the green, and people speak. But when everybody knows everybody else's business . . . I don't know. (*Pause.*) You can't kick a cow in Leenane without some bastard holding a grudge twenty year.

Maureen   It's true enough.

Pato   It is. In England they don't care if you live or die, and it's funny but that isn't altogether a bad thing. Ah, sometimes it is . . . ah, I don't know.

Maureen (*pause*)   Do you think you'll ever settle down in the one place so, Pato? When you get married, I suppose.

Pato (*half-laughing*)   'When I get married . . .'

Maureen   You will someday, I'll bet you, get married. Wouldn't you want to?

Pato   I can't say it's something I do worry me head over.

Maureen   Of course, the rake of women you have stashed all over, you wouldn't need to.

Pato (*smiling*)   I have no rake of women.

Maureen   You have one or two, I bet.

Pato   I may have one or two. That I know to say hello to, now.

Maureen   Hello me . . . A-hole.

Pato   Is true. (*Pause.*) Sure, I'm no . . .

Maureen (*pause*)   No what?

Pause. **Pato** *shrugs and shakes his head, somewhat sadly. Pause. The song 'The Spinning Wheel', sung by Delia Murphy, has just started on the radio.*

Maureen (*continued*) Me mother does love this oul song. Oul Delia Murphy.

Pato This is a creepy oul song.

Maureen It *is* a creepy oul song.

Pato She does have a creepy oul voice. Always scared me this song did when I was a lad. She's like a ghoul singing. (*Pause.*) Does the grandmother die at the end, now, or is she just sleeping?

Maureen Just sleeping, I think she is.

Pato Aye ...

Maureen (*pause*) While the two go hand in hand through the fields.

Pato Aye.

Maureen Be moonlight.

Pato (*nods*) They don't write songs like that any more. Thank Christ. (**Maureen** *laughs. Brighter.*) Wasn't it a grand night though, Maureen, now?

Maureen It was.

Pato Didn't we send them on their way well?

Maureen We did, we did.

Pato Not a dry eye.

Maureen Indeed.

Pato Eh?

Maureen Indeed.

Pato Aye. That we did. That we did.

Maureen (*pause*) So who *was* the Yankee girl you did have your hands all over?

Pato (*laughing*)   Oh, will you stop it with your 'hands all over'?! Barely touched her, I did.

Maureen   Oh-ho!

Pato   A second cousin of me uncle, I think she is. Dolores somebody. Healey or Hooley. Healey. Boston, too, she lives.

Maureen   That was illegal so if it's your second cousin she is.

Pato   Illegal me arse, and it's not *my* second cousin she is anyway, and what's so illegal? Your second cousin's boobs aren't out of bounds, are they?

Maureen   They are!

Pato   I don't know about that. I'll have to consult with me lawyer on that one. I may get arrested the next time. And I have a defence anyways. She had dropped some Taytos on her blouse, there, I was just brushing them off for her.

Maureen   Taytos me arsehole, Pato Dooley!

Pato   Is true! (*Lustful pause. Nervously.*) Like this is all it was . . .

Pato *slowly reaches out and gently brushes at, then gradually fondles,* **Maureen**'s *breasts. She caresses his hand as he's doing so, then slowly gets up and sits across his lap, fondling his head as he continues touching her.*

Maureen   She was prettier than me.

Pato   You're pretty.

Maureen   She was prettier.

Pato   I like you.

Maureen   You have blue eyes.

Pato   I do.

Maureen   Stay with me tonight.

Pato   I don't know, now, Maureen.

Maureen   Stay. Just tonight.

Pato (*pause*)   Is your mother asleep?

Maureen I don't care if she is or she isn't. (*Pause*.) Go lower.

Pato *begins easing his hands down her front.*

Maureen Go lower ... Lower ...

His hands reach her crotch. She tilts her head back slightly. The song on the radio ends. Blackout.

Scene Four

Morning. **Maureen**'s *black dress is lying across the table.* **Mag** *enters from the hall carrying a potty of urine, which she pours out down the sink. She exits into the hall to put the potty away and returns a moment later, wiping her empty hands on the sides of her nightie. She spots the black dress and picks it up disdainfully.*

Mag Forty pounds just for that skimpy dress? That dress is just skimpy. And laying it around then?

She tosses the dress into a far corner, returns to the kitchen and switches the kettle on, speaking loudly to wake **Maureen**.

I suppose I'll have to be getting me own Complan too, the hour you dragged yourself in whatever time it was with your oul dress. (*Quietly*.) That dress just looks silly. (*Loudly*.) Go the whole hog and wear no dress would be nearer the mark! (*Quietly*.) Snoring the head off you all night. Making an oul woman get her Complan, not to mention her porridge. Well, I won't be getting me own porridge, I'll tell you that now. I'd be afeard. You won't catch me getting me own porridge. Oh no. You won't be catching me out so easily.

Pato *has just entered from the hall, dressed in trousers and pulling on a shirt.*

Pato Good morning there, now, Mrs.

Mag *is startled, staring at* **Pato** *dumbfounded.*

Mag Good morning there, now.

Pato Is it porridge you're after?

Mag It is.

Pato   I'll be getting your porridge for you, so, if you like.

Mag   Oh-h.

Pato   Go ahead and rest yourself.

*Mag sits in the rocking chair, keeping her eyes on **Pato** all the while as he prepares her porridge.*

Pato   It's many the time I did get me brother his porridge of a school morning, so I'm well accustomed. (*Pause.*) You couldn't make it to the oul Yanks' do yesterday so?

Mag   No.

Pato   Your bad hip it was, Maureen was saying.

Mag (*still shocked*)   Aye, me bad hip. (*Pause.*) Where's Maureen, now?

Pato   Em, having a lie-in a minute or two, she is. (*Pause.*) To tell you the truth, I was all for . . . I was all for creeping out before ever you got yourself up, but Maureen said 'Aren't we all adults, now? What harm?' I suppose we are, but . . . I don't know. It's still awkward, now, or something. D'you know what I mean? I don't know. (*Pause.*) The Yanks'll be touching down in Boston about now anyways. God willing anyways. Aye. (*Pause.*) A good oul send-off we gave them anyways, we did, to send them off. Aye. (*Pause.*) Not a dry eye. (*Pause.*) Aye. (*Pause.*) Was it a mug of Complan too you wanted?

Mag   It was.

Pato fixes her Complan and brings it over.

Pato   You like your Complan so.

Mag   I don't.

Pato   Do you not, now?

Mag   She makes me drink it when I don't like it and forces me.

Pato   But Complan's good for you anyways if you're old.

Mag   I suppose it's good for me.

Pato   It is. Isn't it chicken flavour?

Mag   I don't know what flavour.

Pato (*checking box*)   Aye, it's chicken flavour. That's the best flavour.

Pato *returns to the porridge.*

Mag (*quietly*)   With all oul lumps you do make it, never minding flavour. *And* no spoon.

Pato *gives* **Mag** *her porridge and sits at the table.*

Pato   There you go, now. (*Pause.*) Whatever happened to your hand there, Mrs? Red raw, it is.

Mag   Me hand, is it?

Pato   Was it a scould you did get?

Mag   It *was* a scould.

Pato   You have to be careful with scoulds at your age.

Mag   Careful, is it? Uh-huh . . .

Maureen *enters from the hall, wearing only a bra and slip, and goes over to* **Pato**.

Maureen   Careful what? We was careful, weren't we, Pato?

Maureen *sits across* **Pato**'s *lap.*

Pato (*embarrassed*)   Maureen, now . . .

Maureen   Careful enough, cos we don't need any babies coming, do we? We do have enough babies in this house to be going on with.

Maureen *kisses him at length.* **Mag** *watches in disgust.*

Pato   Maureen, now . . .

Maureen   Just thanking you for a wonderful night, I am, Pato. Well worth the wait it was. *Well* worth the wait.

Pato (*embarrassed*)   Good-oh.

Mag   Discussing me scoulded hand we was before you breezed in with no clothes!

Maureen   Ar, feck your scoulded hand. (*To* **Pato**.) You'll have to be putting that thing of yours in me again before too long is past, Pato. I do have a taste for it now, I do . . .

Pato   Maureen . . .

She kisses him, gets off, and stares at **Mag** *as she passes into the kitchen.*

Maureen   A mighty oul taste. Uh-huh.

Pato *gets up and idles around in embarrassment.*

Pato   Em, I'll have to be off now in a minute anyways. I do have packing to do I do, and whatyoucall . . .

Mag (*pointing at* **Maureen**. *Loudly*)   *She*'s the one that scoulded me hand! I'll tell you that, now! Let alone sitting on stray men! Held it down on the range she did! Poured chippan fat o'er it! Aye, and told the doctor it was me!

Maureen (*pause. Nonplussed, to* **Pato**)   Be having a mug of tea before you go, Pato, now.

Pato (*pause*)   Maybe a quick one.

Maureen *pours out the tea.* **Mag** *looks back and forth between the two of them.*

Mag   Did you not hear what I said?!

Maureen   Do you think Pato listens to the smutterings of a senile oul hen?

Mag   Senile, is it? (*She holds up her left hand.*) Don't I have the evidence?

Maureen   Come over here a second, Pato. I want you to smell this sink for me.

Mag   Sinks have nothing to do with it!

Maureen   Come over here now, Pato.

Pato   Eh?

Pato *goes into the kitchen.*

Maureen   Smell that sink.

Pato *leans into the sink, sniffs it, then pulls his head away in disgust.*

Mag   Nothing to do with it, sinks have!

Maureen   Nothing to do with it, is it? Everything to do with it, *I* think it has. Serves as evidence to the character of me accuser, it does.

Pato   What is that, now? The drains?

Maureen   Not the drains at all. Not the drains at all. Doesn't she pour a potty of wee away down there every morning, though I tell her seven hundred times the lavvy to use, but oh no.

Mag   Me scoulded hand this conversation was, and not wee at all!

Maureen   And doesn't even rinse it either. Now is that hygienic? And she does have a urine infection too, is even less hygienic. I wash me praities in there. Here's your tea now, Pato.

Pato *takes his tea, sipping it squeamishly.*

Mag   Put some clothes on you, going around the house half-naked! Would be more in your line!

Maureen   I do like going around the house half-naked. It does turn me on, it does.

Mag   I suppose it does, aye.

Maureen   It does.

Mag   And reminds you of Difford Hall in England, too, I'll bet it does . . .

Maureen (*angrily*)   Now you just shut your fecking . . .

Mag   None of your own clothes they let you wear in there either, did they?

Maureen   Shut your oul gob, I said . . . !

Mag   Only long gowns and buckle-down jackets . . .

Maureen *approaches* **Mag**, *fists clenched.* **Pato** *catches her arm and steps between the two.*

Pato   What's the matter with ye two at all, now . . . ?

Mag   Difford Hall! Difford Hall! Difford Hall ...!

Maureen   Difford Hall, uh-huh. And I suppose ...

Mag   Difford Hall! Difford Hall ...!

Maureen   And I suppose that potty of wee was just a figment of me imagination?

Mag   Forget wee! Forget wee! D'you want to know what Difford Hall is, fella?

Maureen   Shut up, now!

Mag   It's a nut-house! An oul nut-house in England I did have to sign her out of and promise to keep her in me care. Would you want to be seeing the papers now?

Mag *shuffles off to the hall.*

As proof, like. Or to prove am I just a senile oul hen, like, or *who*'s the loopy one? Heh! Pegging wee in me face, oh aye ...

Quiet pause. **Maureen** *idles over to the table and sits.* **Pato** *pours his tea down the sink, rinses his mug and washes his hands.*

Maureen (*quietly*)   It's true I was in a home there a while, now, after a bit of a breakdown I had. Years ago this is.

Pato   What harm a breakdown, sure? Lots of people do have breakdowns.

Maureen   A lot of doolally people, aye.

Pato   Not doolally people at all. A lot of well-educated people have breakdowns too. In fact, if you're well-educated it's even more likely. Poor Spike Milligan, isn't he forever having breakdowns? He hardly stops. I do have trouble with me nerves every now and then, too, I don't mind admitting. There's no shame at all in that. Only means you do think about things, and take them to heart.

Maureen   No shame in being put in a nut-house a month? Ah no.

Pato   No shame in thinking about things and worrying about things, I'm saying, and 'nut-house' is a silly word to be using, and you know that well enough, now, Maureen.

Maureen   I do.

Pato *goes over and sits across the table from her.*

Maureen   In England I was, this happened. Cleaning work. When I was twenty-five. Me first time over. Me only time over. Me sister had just got married, me other sister just about to. Over in Leeds I was, cleaning offices. Bogs. A whole group of us, only them were all English. 'Ya oul backward Paddy fecking . . . The fecking pig's-backside face on ya.' The first time out of Connemara this was I'd been. 'Get back to that backward fecking pigsty of yours or whatever hole it was you drug yourself out of.' Half of the swearing I didn't even understand. I had to have a black woman explain it to me. Trinidad she was from. They'd have a go at her too, but she'd just laugh. This big face she had, this big oul smile. And photos of Trinidad she'd show me, and 'What the hell have you left there for?' I'd say. 'To come to this place, cleaning shite?' And a calendar with a picture of Connemara on I showed her one day, and 'What the hell have you left there for?' she said back to me. 'To come to this place . . . ' (*Pause.*) But she moved to London then, her husband was dying. And after that it all just got to me.

Pato (*pause*)   That's all past and behind you now anyways, Maureen.

Pause. **Maureen** *looks at him a while.*

Maureen   Am I still a nut case you're saying, or you're wondering?

Pato   Not at all, now . . .

Maureen   Oh no . . . ?

Maureen *gets up and wanders back to the kitchen.*

Pato   Not at all. That's a long time in the past is all I'm saying. And nothing to be ashamed of. Put it behind you, you should.

Maureen   Put it behind me, aye, with that one hovering eyeing me every minute, like I'm some kind of . . . some kind of . . . (*Pause.*) And, no, I didn't scould her oul hand, no matter how doolally I ever was. Trying to cook chips on her own, she was. We'd argued, and I'd left her on her own an hour, and chips she up and decided she wanted. She must've tipped the pan over. God knows how, the eej. I just found her lying there. Only, because of Difford Hall, she thinks any accusation she throws at me I won't be any the wiser. I won't be able to tell the differ, what's true and what's not. Well, I *am* able to tell the differ. Well able, the smelly oul bitch.

Pato   You shouldn't let her get to you, Maureen.

Maureen   How can I help it, Pato? She's enough to drive anyone loopy, if they weren't loopy to begin with.

Pato (*smiling*)   She is at that, I suppose.

Maureen (*smiling*)   She is. It's surprised I am how sane I've turned out!

They both smile. Pause.

Pato   I *will* have to be off in a minute now, Maureen.

Maureen   Okay, Pato. Did you finish your tea, now?

Pato   I didn't. The talk of your mother's wee, it did put me off it.

Maureen   It would. It would anybody. Don't I have to live with it? (*Sadly.*) Don't I have to live with it? (*Looking straight at him.*) I suppose I do, now.

Pato (*pause*)   Be putting on some clothes there, Maureen. You'll freeze with no fire down.

Pause. **Maureen**'s *mood has become sombre again. She looks down at herself.*

Maureen (*quietly*)   'Be putting on some clothes'? Is it ugly you think I am now, so, 'Be putting on some clothes ...'

Pato   No, Maureen, the cold, I'm saying. You can't go walking about ... You'll freeze, sure.

Maureen   It wasn't ugly you thought I was last night, or maybe it was, now.

Pato   No, Maureen, now. What ...?

Maureen   A beauty queen you thought I was last night, or you said I was. When it's 'Cover yourself', now, 'You do sicken me' . . .

Pato (*approaching her*)   Maureen, no, now, what are you saying that for . . . ?

Maureen   Maybe that was the reason so.

Pato (*stops*)   The reason what?

Maureen   Be off with you so, if I sicken you.

Pato   You don't sicken me.

Maureen (*almost crying*)   Be off with you, I said.

Pato (*approaching again*)   Maureen . . .

Mag *enters, waving papers, stopping* **Pato**'*s approach.*

Mag   Eh? Here's the papers now, Difford Hall, if I'm such a senile oul hen. Eh? Who wants an oul read, now? Eh? Proof this is, let alone pegging sinks at me! (*Pause.*) Eh?

Pato   Maureen . . .

Maureen (*composed. Gently*)   Be going now, Pato.

Pato (*pause*)   I'll write to you from England. (*Pause. Sternly.*) Look at me! (*Pause. Softly.*) I'll write to you from England.

Pato *puts on his jacket, turns for a last look at* **Maureen**, *then exits, closing the door behind him. Footsteps away. Pause.*

Mag   He won't write at all. (*Pause.*) And I did throw your oul dress in that dirty corner too!

Pause. **Maureen** *looks at her a moment, sad, despairing but not angry.*

Maureen   Why? Why? Why do you . . . ?

Pause. **Maureen** *goes over to where her dress is lying, crouches down beside it and picks it up, holding it to her chest. She lingers there a moment, then gets up and passes her mother.*

Just look at yourself.

Maureen *exits into hall.*

Mag Just look at *your*self too, would be . . . would be . . .
(**Maureen** *shuts the hall door behind her.*) . . . more in your line.

Mag *is still holding up the papers rather dumbly. Pause. She lays the
papers down, scratches herself, notices her uneaten porridge and sticks a
finger in it. Quietly.*

Me porridge is gone cold now. (*Loudly.*) Me porridge is gone
cold now!

Mag *stares out front, blankly. Blackout.*

Interval.

Scene Five

Most of the stage is in darkness apart from a spotlight or some such on
Pato *sitting at the table as if in a bedsit in England, reciting a letter he
has written to* **Maureen.**

Pato Dear Maureen, it is Pato Dooley and I'm writing from
London, and I'm sorry it's taken so long to write to you but to
be honest I didn't know whether you wanted me to one way or
the other, so I have taken it upon myself to try and see. There
are a lot of things I want to say but I am no letter-writer but I
will try to say them if I can. Well, Maureen, there is no major
news here, except a Wexford man on the site a day ago, a rake
of bricks fell on him from the scaffold and forty stitches he did
have in his head and was lucky to be alive at all, he was an old
fella, or fifty-odd anyways, but apart from that there is no
major news. I do go out for a pint of a Saturday or a Friday but
I don't know nobody and don't speak to anyone. There is no
one to speak to. The gangerman does pop his head in
sometimes. I don't know if I've spelt it right, 'Gangerman', is
it 'e-r' or is it 'a'? It is not a word we was taught in school. Well,
Maureen, I am 'beating around the bush' as they say, because
it is you and me I do want to be talking about, if there is such a
thing now as 'you and me', I don't know the state of play.
What I thought I thought we were getting on royally, at the
goodbye to the Yanks and the part after when we did talk and

went to yours. And I *did* think you were a beauty queen and I *do* think, and it wasn't anything to do with that at all or with you at all, I think you thought it was. All it was, it has happened to me a couple of times before when I've had a drink taken and was nothing to do with did I want to. I would have been honoured to be the first one you chose, and flattered, and the thing that I'm saying, I was honoured then and I am still honoured, and just because it was not to be that night, does it mean it is not to be ever? I don't see why it should, and I don't see why you was so angry when you was so nice to me when it happened. I think you thought I looked at you differently when your breakdown business came up, when I didn't look at you differently at all, or the thing I said 'Put on your clothes, it's cold', when you seemed to think I did not want to be looking at you in your bra and slip there, when nothing could be further from the truth, because if truth be told I could have looked at you in your bra and slip until the cows came home. I could never get my fill of looking at you in your bra and slip, and some day, God-willing, I will be looking at you in your bra and slip again. Which leads me on to my other thing, unless you still haven't forgiven me, in which case we should just forget about it and part as friends, but if you *have* forgiven me it leads me on to my other thing which I was lying to you before when I said I had no news because I do have news. What the news is I have been in touch with me uncle in Boston and the incident with the Wexford man with the bricks was just the final straw. You'd be lucky to get away with your life the building sites in England, let alone the bad money and the 'You oul Irish this-and-that', and I have been in touch with me uncle in Boston and a job he has offered me there, and I am going to take him up on it. Back in Leenane two weeks tomorrow I'll be, to collect up my stuff and I suppose a bit of a do they'll throw me, and the thing I want to say to you is do you want to come with me? Not straight away of course, I know, because you would have things to clear up, but after a month or two I'm saying, but maybe you haven't forgiven me at all and it's being a fool I'm being. Well, if you haven't forgiven me I suppose it'd be best if we just kept out of each other's way the few days I'm over and if I don't hear from you

I will understand, but if you *have* forgiven me what's to keep
you in Ireland? There's your sisters could take care of your
mother and why should you have had the burden all these
years, don't you deserve a life? And if they say no, isn't there
the home in Oughterard isn't it ideal but they do take good care
of them, my mother before she passed, and don't they have
bingo and what good to your mother does that big hill do? No
good. (*Pause.*) Anyways, Maureen, I will leave it up to you.
My address is up the top there and the number of the phone in
the hall, only let it ring a good while if you want to ring and
you'll need the codes, and it would be grand to hear from you.
If I don't hear from you, I will understand. Take good care of
yourself, Maureen. And that night we shared, even if nothing
happened, it still makes me happy just to think about it, being
close to you, and even if I never hear from you again I'll
always have a happy memory of that night, and that's all I
wanted to say to you. Do think about it. Yours sincerely, Pato
Dooley.

Spotlight cuts out, but while the stage is in darkness **Pato** *continues with
a letter to his brother.*

Dear Raymond, how are you? I'm enclosing a bunch of letters
I don't want different people snooping in on. Will you hand
them out for me and don't be reading them, I know you won't
be. The one to Mick Dowd you can wait till he comes out of
hospital. Let me know how he is or have they arrested the lass
who belted him. The one to poor Girleen you can give to her
any time you see her, it is only to tell her to stop falling in love
with priests. But the one to Maureen Folan I want you to go
over there the day you get this and put it in her hand. This is
important now, in her hand put it. Not much other news here.
I'll fill you in on more of the America details nearer the time.
Yes, it's a great thing. Good luck to you, Raymond, and P.S.
Remember now, in Maureen's hand put it. Goodbye.

Scene Six

Afternoon. **Ray** *is standing near the lit range, watching TV, somewhat engrossed, tapping a sealed envelope against his knee now and then.* **Mag** *watches him and the letter from the rocking-chair. Long pause before* **Ray** *speaks.*

Ray   That Wayne's an oul bastard.

Mag   Is he?

Ray   He is. He never stops.

Mag   Oh-h.

Ray   (*pause*)   D'you see Patricia with the hair? Patricia's bad enough, but Wayne's a pure terror. (*Pause.*) I do like *Sons and Daughters*, I do.

Mag   Do ya?

Ray   Everybody's always killing each other and a lot of the girls do have swimsuits. That's the best kind of programme.

Mag   I'm just waiting for the news to come on.

Ray   (*pause*)   You'll have a long wait.

The programme ends. **Ray** *stretches himself.*

That's that then.

Mag   Is the news not next? Ah no.

Ray   No. For God's sake, *A Country Fecking Practice*'s on next. Isn't it Thursday?

Mag   Turn it off, so, if the news isn't on. That's all I do be waiting for.

Ray *turns the TV off and idles around.*

Ray   Six o'clock the news isn't on 'til. (*He glances at his watch. Quietly, irritated.*) Feck, feck, feck, feck, feck, feck, feck, feck, feck. (*Pause.*) You said she'd be home be now, didn't you?

Mag   I did. (*Pause.*) Maybe she got talking to somebody, although she doesn't usually get talking to somebody. She does keep herself to herself.

Ray   I know well she does keep herself to herself. (*Pause.*) Loopy that woman is, if you ask me. Didn't she keep the tennis ball that came off me and Mairtin Hanlon's swingball set and landed in yere fields and wouldn't give it back no matter how much we begged and that was ten years ago and I still haven't forgotten it?

Mag   I do have no comment, as they say.

Ray   Still haven't forgotten it and I never will forget it!

Mag   But wasn't it that you and Mairtin were pegging yere tennis ball at our chickens and clobbered one of them dead is why your ball was in our fields . . . ?

Ray   It was swingball we were playing, Mrs!

Mag   Oh-h.

Ray   Not clobbering at all. Swingball it was. And never again able to play swingball were we. For the rest of our youth, now. For what use is a swingball set without a ball?

Mag   No use.

Ray   No use is right! No use at all. (*Pause.*) *Bitch!*

Mag (*pause*)   Be off and give your letter to me so, Ray, now, and I'll make sure she gets it, and not have you waiting for a lass ruined your swingball set on you.

Ray *thinks about it, tempted, but grudgingly decides against it.*

Ray   I'm under strict instructions now, Mrs.

Mag (*tuts*)   Make me a mug of tea so.

Ray   I'm not making you a mug of tea. Under duress is all I'm here. I'm not skivvying about on top of it.

Mag (*pause*)   Or another bit of turf on the fire put. I'm cold.

Ray   Did I not just say?

Mag   Ah g'wan, Ray. You're a good boy, God bless you.

Sighing, **Ray** *puts the letter – which* **Mag** *stares at throughout – on the table and uses the heavy black poker beside the range to pick some turf up and place it inside, stoking it afterwards.*

Ray Neverminding swingball, I saw her there on the road the other week and I said hello to her and what did she do? She outright ignored me. Didn't even look up.

Mag Didn't she?

Ray And what I thought of saying, I thought of saying, 'Up your oul hole, Mrs', but I didn't say it, I just thought of saying it, but thinking back on it I should've gone ahead and said it and skitter on the bitch!

Mag It would've been good enough for her to say it, up and ignoring you on the road, because you're a good gasur, Ray, fixing me fire for me. Ah, she's been in a foul oul mood lately.

Ray She does wear horrible clothes. And everyone agrees. (*Finished at the range, poker still in hand,* **Ray** *looks over the tea-towel on the back wall.*) 'May you be half an hour in Heaven afore the Devil knows you're dead.'

Mag Aye.

Ray (*funny voice*) 'May you be half an hour in Heaven afore the Devil knows you're dead.'

Mag (*embarrassed laugh*) Aye.

Ray *idles around a little, wielding the poker.*

Ray This is a great oul poker, this is.

Mag Is it?

Ray Good and heavy.

Mag Heavy and long.

Ray Good and heavy and long. A half a dozen coppers you could take out with this poker and barely notice and have not a scratch on it and then clobber them again just for the fun of seeing the blood running out of them. (*Pause.*) Will you sell it to me?

Mag I will not. To go battering the polis?

Ray A fiver.

Mag   We do need it for the fire, sure.

Ray *tuts and puts the poker back beside the range.*

Ray   Sure, that poker's just going to waste in this house.

Ray *idles into the kitchen. Her eye on the letter,* **Mag** *slowly gets out of her chair.*

Ah, I could get a dozen pokers in town just as good if I wanted, and at half the price.

Just as **Mag** *starts her approach to the letter,* **Ray** *returns, not noticing her, idles past and picks the letter back up on his way.* **Mag** *grimaces slightly and sits back down.* **Ray** *opens the front door, glances out to see if* **Maureen** *is coming, then closes it again, sighing.*

A whole afternoon I'm wasting here. (*Pause.*) When I could be at home watching telly.

Ray *sits at the table.*

Mag   You never know, it might be evening before she's ever home.

Ray (*angrily*)   You said three o'clock it was sure to be when I first came in!

Mag   Aye, three o'clock it usually is, oh aye. (*Pause.*) Just sometimes it does be evening. On occasion, like. (*Pause.*) Sometimes it does be *late* evening. (*Pause.*) Sometimes it does be *night*. (*Pause.*) *Morning* it was one time before she . . .

Ray (*interrupting angrily*)   All right, all right! It's thumping you in a minute I'll be!

Mag (*pause*)   I'm only saying now.

Ray   Well, stop saying! (*Sighs. Long pause.*) This house does smell of pee, this house does.

Mag (*pause. Embarrassed*)   Em, cats do get in.

Ray   Do cats get in?

Mag   They do. (*Pause.*) They do go to the sink.

Ray (*pause*)   What do they go to the sink for?

Mag To wee.

Ray To wee? They go to the sink to wee? (*Piss-taking.*) Sure, that's mighty good of them. You do get a very considerate breed of cat up this way so.

Mag (*pause*) I don't know what breed they are.

Pause. **Ray** *lets his head slump down onto the table with a bump, and slowly and rhythmically starts banging his fist down beside it.*

Ray (*droning*) I don't want to be here, I don't want to be here, I don't want to be here, I don't want to be here ...

Ray *lifts his head back up, stares at the letter, then starts slowly turning it around, end over end, sorely tempted.*

Mag (*pause*) Do me a mug of tea, Ray. (*Pause.*) Or a mug of Complan do me, even. (*Pause.*) And give it a good stir to get rid of the oul lumps.

Ray If it was getting rid of oul lumps I was to be, it wouldn't be with Complan I'd be starting. It would be much closer to home, boy. Oh aye, much closer. A big lump sitting in an oul fecking rocking-chair it would be. I'll tell you that!

Mag (*pause*) Or a Cup-a-Soup do me.

Ray *grits his teeth and begins breathing in and out through them, almost crying.*

Ray (*giving in sadly*) Pato, Pato, Pato. (*Pause.*) Ah what news could it be? (*Pause. Sternly.*) Were I to leave this letter here with you, Mrs, it would be straight to that one you would be giving it, isn't that right?

Mag It is. Oh, straight to Maureen I'd be giving it.

Ray (*pause*) And it isn't opening it you would be?

Mag It is not. Sure, a letter is a private thing. If it isn't my name on it, what business would it be of mine?

Ray And may God strike you dead if you do open it?

Mag And may God strike me dead if I do open it, only He'll have no need to strike me dead because I won't be opening it.

Ray (*pause*)   I'll leave it so.

Ray *stands, places the letter up against a salt-cellar, thinks about it again for a moment, looks* **Mag** *over a second, looks back at the letter again, thinks once more, then waves a hand in a gesture of tired resignation, deciding to leave it.*

I'll be seeing you then, Mrs.

Mag   Be seeing you, Pato. *Ray*, I mean.

Ray *grimaces at her again and exits through the front door, but leaves it slightly ajar, as he is still waiting outside.* **Mag** *places her hands on the sides of the rocking-chair, about to drag herself up, then warily remembers she hasn't heard* **Ray***'s footsteps away. She lets her hands rest back in her lap and sits back serenely. Pause. The front door bursts open and* **Ray** *sticks his head around it to look at her. She smiles at him innocently.*

Ray   Good-oh.

Ray *exits again, closing the door behind him fully this time.* **Mag** *listens to his footsteps fading away, then gets up, picks up the envelope and opens it, goes back to the range and lifts off the lid so that the flames are visible, and stands there reading the letter. She drops the first short page into the flames as she finishes it, then starts reading the second. Slow fade-out.*

Scene Seven

Night. **Mag** *is in her rocking-chair,* **Maureen** *at the table, reading. The radio is on low, tuned to a request show. The reception is quite poor, wavering and crackling with static. Pause before* **Mag** *speaks.*

Mag   A poor reception.

Maureen   Can I help it if it's a poor reception?

Mag (*pause*)   Crackly. (*Pause.*) We can hardly hear the tunes. (*Pause.*) We can hardly hear what are the dedications or from what part of the country.

Maureen   I can hear well enough.

Mag Can ya?

Maureen (*pause*)   Maybe it's deaf it is you're going.

Mag   It's not deaf I'm going. Not nearly deaf.

Maureen   It's a home for deaf people I'll have to be putting you in soon. (*Pause.*) And it isn't cod in butter sauce you'll be getting in there. No. Not by a long chalk. Oul beans on toast or something is all you'll be getting in there. If you're lucky. And then if you don't eat it, they'll give you a good kick, or maybe a punch.

Mag (*pause*)   I'd die before I'd let meself be put in a home.

Maureen   Hopefully, aye.

Mag (*pause*)   That was a nice bit of cod in butter sauce, Maureen.

Maureen   I suppose it was.

Mag   Tasty.

Maureen   All I do is boil it in the bag and snip it with a scissor. I hardly need your compliments.

Mag (*pause*)   Mean to me is all you ever are nowadays.

Maureen   If I am or if I'm not. (*Pause.*) Didn't I buy you a packet of wine gums last week if I'm so mean?

Mag (*pause*)   All because of Pato Dooley you're mean, I suppose. (*Pause.*) Him not inviting you to his oul going-away do tonight.

Maureen   Pato Dooley has his own life to lead.

Mag   Only after one thing that man was.

Maureen   Maybe he was, now. Or maybe it was me who was only after one thing. We do have equality nowadays. Not like in your day.

Mag   There was nothing wrong in my day.

Maureen   Allowed to go on top of a man nowadays, we are. All we have to do is ask. And nice it is on top of a man, too.

Mag   Is it nice now, Maureen?

Maureen (*bemused that* **Mag** *isn't offended*)   It is.

Mag   It does sound nice. Ah, good enough for yourself, now.

Maureen, *still bemused, gets some shortbread fingers from the kitchen and eats a couple.*

Mag   And not worried about having been put in the family way, are you?

Maureen   I'm not. We was careful.

Mag   Was ye careful?

Maureen   Aye. We was nice and careful. We was *lovely* and careful, if you must know.

Mag   I'll bet ye was lovely and careful, aye. Oh aye. Lovely and careful, I'll bet ye were.

Maureen (*pause*)   You haven't been sniffing the paraffin lamps again?

Mag (*pause*)   It's always the paraffin lamp business you do throw at me.

Maureen   It's a funny oul mood you're in so.

Mag   Is it a funny oul mood? No. Just a normal mood, now.

Maureen   It's a funny one. (*Pause.*) Aye, a great oul time me and Pato did have. I can see now what all the fuss did be about, but ah, there has to be more to a man than just being good in bed. Things in common too you do have to have, y'know, like what books do you be reading, or what are your politics and the like, so I did have to tell him it was no-go, no matter how good in bed he was.

Mag   When was this you did tell him?

Maureen   A while ago it was I did tell him. Back . . .

Mag (*interrupting*)   And I suppose he was upset at that.

Maureen   He *was* upset at that but I assured him it was for the best and he did seem to accept it then.

Mag I'll bet he accepted it.

Maureen (*pause*) But that's why I thought it would be unfair of me to go over to his do and wish him goodbye. I thought it would be awkward for him.

Mag It would be awkward for him, aye, I suppose. Oh aye. (*Pause.*) So all it was was ye didn't have enough things in common was all that parted ye?

Maureen Is all it was. And parted on amicable terms, and with no grudges on either side. (*Pause.*) No. No grudges at all. I did get what I did want out of Pato Dooley that night, and that was good enough for him, and that was good enough for me.

Mag Oh aye, now. I'm sure. It was good enough for the both of ye. Oh aye.

Mag *smiles and nods.*

Maureen (*laughing*) It's a crazy oul mood you're in for yourself tonight! Pleased that tonight it is Pato's leaving and won't be coming pawing me again is what it is, I bet.

Mag Maybe that's what it is. I *am* glad Pato's leaving.

Maureen (*smiling*) An interfering oul biddy is all you are. (*Pause.*) Do you want a shortbread finger?

Mag I *do* want a shortbread finger.

Maureen Please.

Mag Please.

Maureen *gives* **Mag** *a shortbread finger, after waving it phallically in the air a moment.*

Maureen Remind me of something, shortbread fingers do.

Mag I suppose they do, now.

Maureen   I suppose it's so long since you've seen what they remind me of, you do forget what they look like.

Mag   I suppose I do. And I suppose you're the expert.

Maureen   I am the expert.

Mag   Oh aye.

Maureen   I'm the king of the experts.

Mag   I suppose you are, now. Oh, I'm sure. I suppose you're the king of the experts.

Maureen (*pause. Suspicious*)   Why wouldn't you be sure?

Mag   With your Pato Dooley and your throwing it all in me face like an oul peahen, eh? When . . . (**Mag** *catches herself before revealing any more.*)

Maureen (*pause. Smiling*)   When what?

Mag   Not another word on the subject am I saying. I do have no comment, as they say. This is a nice shortbread finger.

Maureen (*with an edge*)   When what, now?

Mag (*getting scared*)   When nothing, Maureen.

Maureen (*forcefully*)   No, when what, now? (*Pause.*) Have you been speaking to somebody?

Mag   Who would I be speaking to, Maureen?

Maureen (*trying to work it out*)   You've been speaking to somebody. You've . . .

Mag   Nobody have I been speaking to, Maureen. You know well I don't be speaking to anybody. And, sure, who would Pato be telling about that . . . ?

Mag *suddenly realises what she's said.* **Maureen** *stares at her in dumb shock and hate, then walks to the kitchen, dazed, puts a chip-pan on the stove, turns it on high and pours a half-bottle of cooking oil into it, takes down the rubber gloves that are hanging on the back wall and puts them on.* **Mag** *puts her hands on the arms of the rocking-chair to drag herself up, but* **Maureen** *shoves a foot against her stomach and groin, ushering her back.* **Mag** *leans back into the chair, frightened, staring at*

Maureen, *who sits at the table, waiting for the oil to boil. She speaks quietly, staring straight ahead.*

Maureen   How do you know?

Mag   Nothing do I know, Maureen.

Maureen   Uh-huh?

Mag (*pause*)   Or was it Ray did mention something? Aye, I think it was Ray . . .

Maureen   Nothing to Ray would Pato've said about that subject.

Mag (*tearfully*)   Just to stop you bragging like an oul peahen, was I saying, Maureen. Sure what does an oul woman like me know? Just guessing, I was.

Maureen   You know sure enough, and guessing me arse, and not on me face was it written. For the second time and for the last time I'll be asking, now. How do you know?

Mag   On your face it *was* written, Maureen. Sure that's the only way I knew. You still do have the look of a virgin about you you always have had. (*Without malice.*) You always will.

Pause. The oil has started boiling. **Maureen** *rises, turns the radio up, stares at* **Mag** *as she passes her, takes the pan off the boil and turns the gas off, and returns to* **Mag** *with it.*

(*Terrified.*) A letter he did send you I read!

Maureen *slowly and deliberately takes her mother's shrivelled hand, holds it down on the burning range, and starts slowly pouring some of the hot oil over it, as* **Mag** *screams in pain and terror.*

Maureen   Where is the letter?

Mag (*through screams*)   I did burn it! I'm sorry, Maureen!

Maureen   What did the letter say?

Mag *is screaming so much that she can't answer.* **Maureen** *stops pouring the oil and releases the hand, which* **Mag** *clutches to herself, doubled-up, still screaming, crying and whimpering.*

Maureen   What did the letter say?

Mag Said he did have too much to drink, it did! Is why, and not your fault at all.

Maureen And what else did it say?

Mag He won't be putting me into no home!

Maureen What are you talking about, no home? What else did it say?!

Mag I can't remember, now, Maureen. I *can't* . . . !

Maureen *grabs* **Mag**'*s hand, holds it down again and repeats the torture.*

Mag No . . . !

Maureen What else did it say?! Eh?!

Mag (*through screams*) Asked you to go to America with him, it did!

Stunned, **Maureen** *releases* **Mag**'*s hand and stops pouring the oil.* **Mag** *clutches her hand to herself again, whimpering.*

Maureen What?

Mag But how could you go with him? You do still have me to look after.

Maureen (*in a happy daze*) He asked me to go to America with him? Pato asked me to go to America with him?

Mag (*looking up at her*) But what about me, Maureen?

A slight pause before **Maureen**, *in a single and almost lazy motion, throws the considerable remainder of the oil into* **Mag**'*s midriff, some of it splashing up into her face.* **Mag** *doubles-up, screaming, falls to the floor, trying to pat the oil off her, and lies there convulsing, screaming and whimpering.* **Maureen** *steps out of her way to avoid her fall, still in a daze, barely noticing her.*

Maureen (*dreamily, to herself*) He asked me to go to America with him . . . ? (*Recovering herself.*) What time is it? Oh feck, he'll be leaving! I've got to see him. Oh God . . . What will I wear? Uh . . . Me black dress! Me little black dress! It'll be a remembrance to him . . .

Maureen *darts off through the hall.*

Mag (*quietly, sobbing*)   Maureen ... help me ...

Maureen *returns a moment later, pulling her black dress on.*

Maureen (*to herself*)   How do I look? Ah, I'll have to do. What time is it? Oh God ...

Mag   Help me, Maureen ...

Maureen (*brushing her hair*)   Help you, is it? After what you've done? Help you, she says. No, I won't help you, and I'll tell you another thing. If you've made me miss Pato before he goes, then you'll *really* be for it, so you will, and no messing this time. Out of me fecking way, now ...

Maureen *steps over* **Mag**, *who is still shaking on the floor, and exits through the front door. Pause.* **Mag** *is still crawling around slightly. The front door bangs open and* **Mag** *looks up at* **Maureen** *as she breezes back in.*

Me car keys I forgot ...

Maureen *grabs her keys from the table, goes to the door, turns back to the table and switches the radio off.*

Electricity.

Maureen *exits again, slamming the door. Pause. Sound of her car starting and pulling off. Pause.*

Mag (*quietly*)   But who'll look after me, so?

Mag, *still shaking, looks down at her scalded hand. Blackout.*

Scene Eight

Same night. The only light in the room emanates from the orange coals through the grill of the range, just illuminating the dark shapes of **Mag**, *sitting in her rocking-chair, which rocks back and forth of its own volition, her body unmoving, and* **Maureen**, *still in her black dress, who idles very slowly around the room, poker in hand.*

Maureen   To Boston. To Boston I'll be going. Isn't that where them two were from, the Kennedys, or was that somewhere else, now? Robert Kennedy I did prefer over Jack Kennedy. He seemed to be nicer to women. Although I haven't read up on it. (*Pause.*) Boston. It does have a nice ring to it. Better than England it'll be, I'm sure. Although where wouldn't be better than England? No shite I'll be cleaning there, anyways, and no names called, and Pato'll be there to have a say-so anyways if there was to be names called, but I'm sure there won't be. The Yanks do love the Irish. (*Pause.*) Almost begged me, Pato did. Almost on his hands and knees, he was, near enough crying. At the station I caught him, not five minutes to spare, thanks to you. Thanks to your oul interfering. But too late to be interfering you are now. Oh aye. Be far too late, although you did give it a good go, I'll say that for you. Another five minutes and you'd have had it. Poor you. Poor selfish oul bitch, oul you. (*Pause.*) Kissed the face off me, he did, when he saw me there. Them blue eyes of his. Them muscles. Them arms wrapping me. 'Why did you not answer me letter?' And all for coming over and giving you a good kick he was when I told him, but 'Ah no,' I said, 'isn't she just a feeble-minded oul feck, not worth dirtying your boots on?' I was defending you there. (*Pause.*) 'You will come to Boston with me so, me love, when you get up the money.' 'I will, Pato. Be it married or be it living in sin, what do I care? What do I care if tongues'd be wagging? Tongues have wagged about me before, let them wag again. Let them never stop wagging, so long as I'm with you, Pato, what do I care about tongues? So long as it's you and me, and the warmth of us cuddled up, and the skins of us asleep, is all I ever really wanted anyway.' (*Pause.*) 'Except we do still have a problem, what to do with your oul mam, there,' he said. 'Would an oul folks home be too harsh?' 'It wouldn't be too harsh but it would be too expensive.' 'What about your sisters so?' 'Me sisters wouldn't have the bitch. Not even a half-day at Christmas to be with her can them two stand. They clear forgot her birthday this year as well as that. 'How do you stick her without going off your rocker?' they do say to me. Behind her back, like. (*Pause.*) 'I'll leave it up to yourself so,' Pato says. He was on the train be this time, we was kissing out the window, like they do in films. 'I'll leave it up to yourself so, whatever you decide. If it takes a month, let it take a month. And if it's finally you decide you can't bear to be parted from her and have to stay behind, well, I can't say I would like it, but I'd understand. But if even a year it has to take for you to decide, it is a year I will be waiting, and won't be minding the wait.' 'It won't be a year it is you'll be waiting, Pato', I called out then, the train was pulling away. 'It won't be a year nor yet nearly a year. It won't be a week!'

The rocking-chair has stopped its motions. **Mag** *starts to slowly lean forward at the waist until she finally topples over and falls heavily to the floor, dead. A red chunk of skull hangs from a string of skin at the side of her head.* **Maureen** *looks down at her, somewhat bored, taps her on the side with the toe of her shoe, then steps onto her back and stands there in throughtful contemplation.*

'Twas over the stile she did trip. Aye. And down the hill she did fall. Aye. (*Pause.*) Aye.

Pause. Blackout.

Scene Nine

A rainy afternoon. Front door opens and **Maureen** *enters in funeral attire, takes her jacket off and idles around quietly, her mind elsewhere. She lights a fire in the range, turns the radio on low and sits down in the rocking-chair. After a moment she half-laughs, takes down the boxes of Complan and porridge from the kitchen shelf, goes back to the range and empties the contents of both on the fire. She exits into the hall and returns a moment later with an old suitcase which she lays on the table, brushing off a thick layer of dust. She opens it, considers for a second what she needs to pack, then returns to the hall. There is a knock at the door.* **Maureen** *returns, thinks a moment, takes the suitcase off the table and places it to one side, fixes her hair a little, then answers the door.*

Maureen Oh hello there, Ray.

Ray (*off*) Hello there, Mrs ...

Maureen   Come in ahead for yourself.

Ray   I did see you coming ahead up the road.

Ray *enters, closing the door.* **Maureen** *idles to the kitchen and makes herself some tea.*

I didn't think so early you would be back. Did you not want to go on to the reception or the whatyoucall they're having at Rory's so?

Maureen   No. I do have better things to do with me time.

Ray   Aye, aye. Have your sisters gone on to it?

Maureen   They have, aye.

Ray   Of course. Coming back here after, will they be?

Maureen   Going straight home, I think they said they'd be.

Ray   Oh aye. Sure, it's a long oul drive for them. Or fairly long. (*Pause.*) It did all go off okay, then?

Maureen   It did.

Ray   Despite the rain.

Maureen   Despite the rain.

Ray   A poor oul day for a funeral.

Maureen   It was. When it could've been last month we buried her, and she could've got the last of the sun, if it wasn't for the hundred bastarding inquests, proved nothing.

Ray   You'll be glad that's all over and done with now, anyways.

Maureen   Very glad.

Ray   I suppose they do only have their jobs to do. (*Pause.*) Although no fan am I of the bastarding polis. Me two wee toes they went and broke on me for no reason, me arsehole drunk and disorderly.

Maureen   The polis broke your toes, did they?

Ray   They did.

Maureen Oh. Tom Hanlon said what it was you kicked a door in just your socks.

Ray Did he now? And I suppose you believe a policeman's word over mine. Oh aye. Isn't that how the Birmingham Six went down?

Maureen Sure, you can't equate your toes with the Birmingham Six, now, Ray.

Ray It's the selfsame differ. (*Pause.*) What was I saying, now?

Maureen Some bull.

Ray Some bull, is it? No. Asking about your mam's funeral, I was.

Maureen That's what I'm saying.

Ray (*pause*) Was there a big turn-out at it?

Maureen Me sisters and one of their husbands and nobody else but Maryjohnny Rafferty and oul Father Walsh – Welsh – saying the thing.

Ray Father Welsh punched Mairtin Hanlon in the head once, and for no reason. (*Pause.*) Are you not watching telly for yourself, no?

Maureen I'm not. It's only Australian oul shite they do ever show on that thing.

Ray (*slightly bemused*) Sure, that's why I do like it. Who wants to see Ireland on telly?

Maureen *I* do.

Ray All you have to do is look out your window to see Ireland. And it's soon bored you'd be. 'There goes a calf.' (*Pause.*) I be bored anyway. I be continually bored. (*Pause.*) London I'm thinking of going to. Aye. Thinking of it, anyways. To work, y'know. One of these days. Or else Manchester. They have a lot more drugs in Manchester. Supposedly, anyways.

Maureen   Don't be getting messed up in drugs, now, Ray, for yourself. Drugs are terrible dangerous.

Ray   Terrible dangerous, are they? Drugs, now?

Maureen   You know full well they are.

Ray   Maybe they are, maybe they are. But there are plenty of other things just as dangerous, would kill you just as easy. Maybe even easier.

Maureen (*wary*)   Things like what, now?

Ray (*pause. Shrugging*)   This bastarding town for one.

Maureen (*pause. Sadly*)   Is true enough.

Ray   Just that it takes seventy years. Well, it won't take me seventy years. I'll tell you that. No way, boy. (*Pause.*) How old was your mother, now, when she passed?

Maureen   Seventy, aye. Bang on.

Ray   She had a good innings, anyway. (*Pause.*) Or an innings, anyway. (*Sniffs the air.*) What's this you've been burning?

Maureen   Porridge and Complan I've been burning.

Ray   For why?

Maureen   Because I don't eat porridge or Complan. The remainders of me mother's, they were. I was having a good clear-out.

Ray   Only a waste that was.

Maureen   Do I need your say-so so?

Ray   I'd've been glad to take them off your hands, I'm saying.

Maureen (*quietly*)   I don't need your say-so.

Ray   The porridge, anyway. I do like a bit of porridge. I'd've left the Complan. I don't drink Complan. Never had no call to.

Maureen   There's some Kimberleys left in the packet I was about to burn too, you can have, if it's such a big thing.

Ray   I *will* have them Kimberleys. I do love Kimberleys.

Maureen   I bet you do.

Ray *eats a couple of Kimberleys.*

Ray   Are they a bit stale, now? (*Chews.*) It does be hard to tell with Kimberleys. (*Pause.*) I think Kimberleys are me favourite biscuits out of any biscuits. Them or Jaffa Cakes. (*Pause.*) Or Wagon Wheels. (*Pause.*) Or would you classify Wagon Wheels as biscuits at all now. Aren't they more of a kind of a bar . . . ?

Maureen (*interrupting*)   I've things to do now, Ray. Was it some reason you had to come over or was it just to discuss Wagon Wheels?

Ray   Oh aye, now. No, I did have a letter from Pato the other day and he did ask me to come up.

Maureen *sits in the rocking-chair and listens with keen interest.*

Maureen   He did? What did he have to say?

Ray   He said sorry to hear about your mother and all, and his condolences he sent.

Maureen   Aye, aye, aye, and anything else, now?

Ray   That was the main gist of it, the message he said to pass onto you.

Maureen   It had no times or details, now?

Ray   Times or details? No . . .

Maureen   I suppose . . .

Ray   Eh?

Maureen   Eh?

Ray   Eh? Oh, also he said he was sorry he didn't get to see you the night he left, there, he would've liked to've said goodbye. But if that was the way you wanted it, so be it. Although rude, too, I thought that was.

Maureen (*standing, confused*)   I did see him the night he left. At the station, there.

Ray   What station? Be taxicab Pato left. What are you thinking of?

Maureen (*sitting*)   I don't know now.

Ray   Be taxicab Pato left, and sad that he never got your goodbye, although why he wanted your goodbye I don't know. (*Pause.*) I'll tell you this, Maureen, not being harsh, but your house does smell an awful lot nicer now that your mother's dead. I'll say it does, now.

Maureen   Well, isn't that the best? With me thinking I did see him the night he left, there. The train that pulled away.

He looks at her as if she's mad.

Ray   Aye, aye. (*Mumbled, sarcastic.*) Have a rest for yourself. (*Pause.*) Oh, do you know a lass called, em . . . Dolores Hooley, or Healey, now? She was over with the Yanks when they was over.

Maureen   I know the name, aye.

Ray   She was at me uncle's do they had there, dancing with me brother early on. You remember?

Maureen   Dancing with him, was it? Throwing herself at him would be nearer the mark. Like a cheap oul whore.

Ray   I don't know about that, now.

Maureen   Like a cheap oul whore. And where did it get her?

Ray   She did seem nice enough to me, there, now. Big brown eyes she had. And I do like brown eyes, me, I do. Oh aye. Like the lass used to be on *Bosco*. Or I *think* the lass used to be on *Bosco* had brown eyes. We had a black and white telly at that time. (*Pause.*) What was I talking about, now?

Maureen   Something about this Dolores Hooley or whoever she fecking is.

Ray   Oh aye. Herself and Pato did get engaged a week ago, now, he wrote and told me.

Maureen (*shocked*)   Engaged to do what?

Ray   Engaged to get married. What do you usually get engaged for? 'Engaged to do what?' Engaged to eat a bun!

Maureen *is dumbstruck.*

Ray   A bit young for him, I think, but good luck to him. A whirlwind oul whatyoucall. July next year, they're thinking of having it, but I'll have to write and tell him to move it either forward or back, else it'll coincide with the European Championships. I wonder if they'll have the European Championships on telly over there at all? Probably not, now, the Yankee bastards. They don't care about football at all. Ah well. (*Pause.*) It won't be much of a change for her anyways, from Hooley to Dooley. Only one letter. The 'h'. That'll be a good thing. (*Pause.*) Unless it's Healey that she is. I can't remember. (*Pause.*) If it's Healey, it'll be three letters. The 'h', the 'e' and the 'a'. (*Pause.*) Would you want me to be passing any message on, now, when I'm writing, Mrs? I'm writing tomorrow.

Maureen   I get ... I do get confused. Dolores Hooley ... ?

Ray (*pause. Irritated*)   Would you want me to be passing on any message, now, I'm saying?

Maureen (*pause*)   Dolores Hooley ... ?

Ray (*sighing*)   Fecking ... The loons you do get in this house! Only repeating!

Maureen   Who's a loon?

Ray   Who's a loon, she says!

Ray *scoffs and turns away, looking out the window.* **Maureen** *quietly picks up the poker from beside the range and, holding it low at her side, slowly approaches him from behind.*

Maureen (*angrily*)   Who's a loon?!

Ray *suddenly sees something hidden behind a couple of boxes on the inner window ledge.*

Ray (*angrily*)   Well, isn't that fecking just the fecking best yet . . . !

Ray picks up a faded tennis ball with a string sticking out of it from the ledge and spins around to confront **Maureen** *with it, so angry that he doesn't even notice the poker.* **Maureen** *stops in her tracks.*

Sitting on that fecking shelf all these fecking years you've had it, and what good did it do ya?! A tenner that swingball set did cost me poor ma and da and in 1979 that was, when a tenner was a lot of money. The best fecking present I did ever get and only two oul months' play out of it I got before you went and confiscated it on me. What right did you have? What right at all? No right. And just left it sitting there then to fade to fecking skitter. I wouldn't've minded if you'd got some use out of it, if you'd taken the string out and played pat-ball or something agin a wall, but no. Just out of pure spite is the only reason you kept it, and right under me fecking nose. And then you go wondering who's a fecking loon? Who's a fecking loon, she says. I'll tell you who's a fecking loon, lady. *You're* a fecking loon!

Maureen *lets the poker fall to the floor with a clatter and sits in the rocking-chair, dazed.*

Maureen   I don't know why I did keep your swingball on you, Raymond. I can't remember at all, now. I think me head was in a funny oul way in them days.

Ray   'In them days,' she says, as she pegs a good poker on the floor and talks about trains.

Ray picks the poker up and puts it in its place.

That's a good poker, that is. Don't be banging it against anything hard like that, now.

Maureen   I won't.

Ray   That's an awful good poker. (*Pause.*) To show there's no hard feelings over me swingball, will you sell me that poker, Mrs? A fiver I'll give you.

Maureen   Ah, I don't want to be selling me poker now, Ray.

Ray G'wan. Six!

Maureen No. It does have sentimental value to me.

Ray I don't forgive you, so!

Maureen Ah, don't be like that, now, Ray . . .

Ray No, I don't forgive you at all . . .

Ray *goes to the front door and opens it.*

Maureen Ray! Are you writing to your brother, so?

Ray (*sighing*) I am. Why?

Maureen Will you be passing a message on from me?

Ray (*sighs*) Messages, messages, messages, messages! What's the message, so? And make it a short one.

Maureen Just say . . .

Maureen *thinks about it a while.*

Ray This week, if you can!

Maureen Just say . . . Just say, 'The beauty queen of Leenane says hello.' That's all.

Ray 'The beauty queen of Leenane says hello.'

Maureen Aye. No!

Ray *sighs again.*

Maureen *Goodbye.* Goodbye. 'The beauty queen of Leenane says *goodbye.*'

Ray 'The beauty queen of Leenane says goodbye.' Whatever the feck that means, I'll pass it on. 'The beauty queen of Leenane says goodbye', although after this fecking swingball business, I don't see why the feck I should. Goodbye to you so, Mrs . . .

Maureen Will you turn the radio up a biteen too, before you go, there, Pato, now? *Ray*, I mean . . .

Ray (*exasperated*) Feck . . .

Ray *turns the radio up.*

The exact fecking image of your mother you are, sitting there pegging orders and forgetting me name! Goodbye!

Maureen And pull the door after you . . .

Ray (*shouting angrily*) I was going to pull the fecking door after me!!

Ray *slams the door behind him as he exits. Pause.* **Maureen** *starts rocking slightly in the chair, listening to the song by The Chieftains on the radio. The announcer's quiet, soothing voice is then heard.*

Announcer A lovely tune from The Chieftains there. This next one, now, goes out from Annette and Margo Folan to their mother Maggie, all the way out in the mountains of Leenane, a lovely part of the world there, on the occasion of her seventy-first birthday last month now. Well, we hope you had a happy one, Maggie, and we hope there'll be a good many more of them to come on top of it. I'm sure there will. This one's for you, now.

'The Spinning Wheel' by Delia Murphy is played. **Maureen** *gently rocks in the chair until about the middle of the fourth verse, when she quietly gets up, picks up the dusty suitcase, caresses it slightly, moves slowly to the hall door and looks back at the empty rocking-chair a while. It is still rocking gently. Slight pause, then* **Maureen** *exits into the hall, closing its door behind her as she goes. We listen to the song on the radio to the end, as the chair gradually stops rocking and the lights, very slowly, fade to black.*

A Skull in Connemara

A Skull in Connemara, a Druid Theatre Company/Royal Court Theatre co-production, was first presented at the Town Hall Theatre, Galway, on 3rd June 1997, and subsequently opened at the Royal Court Theatre Downstairs on 17th July 1997. The cast was as follows:

Mick Dowd   Mick Lally
Mary Rafferty   Anna Manahan
Mairtin Hanlon   David Wilmot
Tom Hanlon   Brian F. O'Byrne

Directed by Garry Hynes
Designed by Francis O'Connor
Lighting design by Ben Ormerod
Sound design by Bell Helicopter
Music by Paddy Cunneen

Characters

Mick Dowd, *fifties.*
Maryjohnny Rafferty, *seventies.*
Mairtin Hanlon, *late teens/early twenties.*
Thomas Hanlon, *thirties.*

Setting: Rural Galway.

Scene One

The fairly spartan main room of a cottage in rural Galway. Front door stage left, a table with two chairs and a cupboard towards the right, and a lit fireplace in the centre of the back wall with an armchair on each side of it. A crucifix hangs on the back wall and an array of old farm tools, sickles, scythes and picks etc., hang just below it. At the start of the play, **Mick Dowd***, a man in his fifties whose cottage it is, is sitting in the left armchair as* **Mary Rafferty***, a heavy-set, white-haired neighbour in her seventies, knocks and is let in through the front door.*

Mary   Mick.

Mick   Maryjohnny.

Mary   Cold.

Mick   I suppose it's cold.

Mary   Cold, aye. It's turning.

Mick   Is it turning?

Mary   It's turning now, Mick. The summer is going.

Mick   It isn't going yet, or is it now?

Mary   The summer is going, Mick.

Mick   What month are we now?

Mary   Are we September?

Mick (*thinks*)   We are, d'you know?

Mary   The summer is going.

Mick   What summer we had.

Mary   What summer we had. We had no summer.

Mick   Sit down for yourself, there, Mary.

Mary (*sitting*)   Rain, rain, rain, rain, rain we had. And now the cold. And now the dark closing in. The leaves'll be turning in a couple of weeks, and that'll be the end of it.

Mick   I didn't even know it *was* September, and I'll admit it.

Mary   Did you not now, Mick? What month did you think it was?

Mick   August or something I thought it was.

Mary   August? (*Laughs.*) August is gone.

Mick   I know it is, now.

Mary   August went.

Mick   I know it did.

Mary   Last month August was.

Mick (*slightly irritated*)   I know it was now, Mary. You don't have to keep saying.

Mary (*pause*)   Didn't the boys and girls go back to school, and stopped parading up and down the street like . . .

Mick   Ah sure they did. And don't I usually notice that one, and say to meself, 'The boys and girls have gone back to school. The summer is surely over now.'

Mary   Like a pack o' whores.

Mick (*pause*)   Who's like a pack o' whores?

Mary   Them schoolies parading up and down.

Mick   I wouldn't say a pack o' whores, now.

Mary   Kissing.

Mick   What harm?

Mary   Cursing.

Mick   Mary, you're too old-fashioned, so you are. Who doesn't curse nowadays?

Mary   I don't.

Mick   'You don't.'

Mary (*pause*) Eamonn Andrews didn't.

Mick Well we can't all be as good as you or Eamonn Andrews. And I'll bet Eamonn Andrews would've cursed too were he to've fell, or sat on a nail.

Mary He would not.

Mick It's only on television you ever saw. When he got home he probably cursed a-plenty. He probably did nothing but curse.

Mary Oh, a lie now . . .

Mick When he got home now, I'm saying.

Mary I'll tell you someone else who doesn't curse. (*Pointing to the crucifix.*) That man doesn't curse.

Mick Well we can't all be as good as Our Lord. Let alone Eamonn Andrews. Now those youngsters are only out for a bit of fun during their holidays, and not meaning no harm to anybody.

Mary No harm to anybody, is it, Mick? And the three I caught weeing in the churchyard and when I told them I'd tell Father Cafferty, what did they call me? A fat oul biddy!

Mick I know they did, Mary, and they shouldn't't've . . .

Mary I know well they shouldn't't've!'

Mick That was twenty-seven years ago for God's sake, Mary.

Mary Twenty-seven years ago or not!

Mick You should let bygones be bygones.

Mary Bygones, is it? No, I will not let bygones be bygones. I'll tell you when I'll let bygones be bygones. When I see them burned in Hell I'll let bygones be bygones, and not before!

Mick Hell is too harsh a price just for weeing. Sure they were only five, God bless them.

Mary   On consecrated ground, Mick.

Mick   On consecrated ground or not. They may have been bursting. And what's consecrated ground anyways but any old ground with a dab of holy water pegged on it?

Mary   Well, you would be the man, Mick Dowd, I'd expect would argue that, the filthy occupation you take on every autumntime . . .

Mick (*interrupting*)   There's no need for that.

Mary   Is there no need for that, now?

Mick *gets up, pours out two glasses of poteen, gives one to* **Mary** *and sits down with the other.*

Mick   Doesn't the County pay for the job to be done if it's such a filthy occupation? Doesn't the priest half the time stand over me and chat to me and bring me cups of tea? Eh?

Mary (*pause*)   I suppose he does. (*Sips her poteen.*) Not that I'd give a bent ha'penny for that young skitter.

Mick   What young skitter?

Mary   Father Welsh, Walsh, Welsh.

Mick   Nothing the matter with Father Welsh.

Mary   Nothing the matter at all, except I don't too much like going to confession with a gasur aged two!

Mick   What the Hell sins do you have to confess to him every week anyways?

Mary   What sins do *you* confess would be more in your line.

Mick (*playfully*)   What would it be, now? It wouldn't be impure thoughts? Ah no. It must be 'Thou shalt not steal' so.

Mary   How, 'Thou shalt not steal'?

Mick   Oh, cadging off the Yanks a pound a throw the

maps the Tourist Board asked you to give them for free.
Telling them your Liam's place was where *The Quiet Man*
was filmed, when wasn't it a hundred miles away in Ma'am
Cross or somewhere?

Mary   A hundred miles is it? Ma'am Cross has moved so,
because eight miles it was the last time I looked.

Mick   John Wayne photos, two pound a pop. Maureen
O'Hara drank out of this mug – a fiver. Boy, I'll tell you,
anh? Them eejit Yanks.

Mary   If the eejit Yanks want to contribute a couple of
bob to an oul lady's retirement, I'll not be standing in their
way, sure.

Mick   So if it's not cadging off them thicks you confess it
must be playing the ten books the bingo, so.

Mary (*smiling*)   I don't play ten books the bingo.

Mick   Oh, the County could round up a hundred
witnesses would tell you the differ, 'cos twenty year it's
been going on now.

Mary   Maybe now and then I do forget how many books
I've picked up . . .

Mick   Forget, is it?

Mary (*slightly hurt*)   It's forget, Mick. I do mean to pick up
the four, and then two books get stuck together, and before
I know where I am I'm sitting down and how many books
do I have . . .

Mick   Mary Rafferty, you have played ten books in that
church hall for every week since de Valera was twelve, and
it's ten books if they're lucky, because doesn't it rise to
fifteen when the Christmas jackpot draws on, and isn't it
twenty-two books at once your Guinness World's record is,
and wouldn't it be higher still if it wasn't eighteen times
you won that night and you thought they might begin to
get suspicious?

Mary *stares at him angrily.*

Mary Well on the subject of confession, now, Mick Dowd, how long is it since *you've* seen the priest? Seven and a half years, is it, Mick?

Mick Eh?

Mary Seven and a half . . .

Mick (*angrily*) That's enough of that, now, Mary.

Mary Wasn't it your Oona used to drag you there of a week . . . ?

Mick (*angrily, standing*) That's enough of that now, I said! Or else be off with you!

He idles a little, pouring himself another drink.

Mary He calls too slow anyways.

Mick Who calls too slow?

Mary That skitter at St Patrick's the bingo.

Mick Oh, calls the bingo.

Mary Walsh, Welsh. (*Pause.*) You need ten books to make it worthwhile, else you'd be hanging about, so. It isn't to win I have ten books.

Mick It's the game of it.

Mary It's the game of it, Mick, is right.

Mick Nobody begrudges you anyways.

Mary Because I'm oul.

Mick Nobody begrudges you still.

A knock at the front door, which pushes open immediately. **Mairtin** *enters in a Man. Utd away shirt, blowing bubbles now and then.*

Mairtin How is all?

Mary How are you, Mairtin?

Mick How are you, Mairtin? And close the door.

Mairtin   I'll close the door (*Does so.*) or was it a barn with a wide open door you were born in, me mam says. She says, was it a barn with a wide open door you were born in, Mary beag, and I say 'You're the get would know, Mam.'

Mary *tuts.*

Mairtin   No, I say, you're the woman would know, Mam. I do. That's what I say, like. Because if anybody was to know where I was born, wouldn't it be her? (*Pause.*) The Regional Hospital I was born. In Galway.

Mick   We know where the Regional Hospital is.

Mairtin   Aye. (*To* **Mary**.) Wasn't it you was in there with your hip?

Mary   No.

Mairtin   It must've been somebody else so. Aye. Who was it? Somebody who fell down and was fat.

Mick   What is it you've come over about, Mairtin?

Mairtin   Father Welsh or Walsh sent me over. It was choir and I was disruptive. Is that poteen, Mick? You wouldn't spare a drop?

Mick   No I wouldn't.

Mairtin   Ah g'wan . . .

Mary   Why was you being disruptive in choir, Mairtin? You used to be a good little singer, God bless you.

Mairtin   Ah, a pack of oul shite they sing now.

Mary *tuts at his language.*

Mairtin   A pack of not very good songs they sing now, I mean. All wailing, and about fishes, and bears.

Mick   About fishes and bears, is it?

Mairtin   It is. That's what *I* said, like. They said no, the youngsters like these ones. What's the song they had us singing tonight? Something about if I was a bear I'd be happy enough, but I'm even more glad I'm human. Ah, a pile of oul wank it is. It's only really the Christmas carols I do like.

Mick   And in September you don't get too much call for them.

Mairtin   Is right, you don't. But I think they should have them all year, instead of the skitter they do, because they do make you very Christmassy, like.

Mary   How is mam and dad, Mairtin, I haven't seen them a few days?

Mairtin   Oh, grand indeed, now. Or anyway me mam's grand and me dad's as grand as a bastard of a get like him can be . . .

Mary   Mairtin. Your own father now.

Mairtin   My own father is right. And if he took his belt off to you for no reason at all eight times a week, it wouldn't be so quick you'd be saying 'Your own father now'. I'll tell you that.

Mick   And you don't do anything to deserve it, I suppose? Ah no.

Mairtin   Not a thing.

Mick   Not a thing, oh aye. Not even the guards' tyres got slashed outside the disco in Carraroe, your pal Ray Dooley got nabbed for, someone else ran away.

Mairtin   Wasn't me now, Mick.

Mick   Oh no. Of course.

Mairtin   I had a bad leg anyways, and what were the guards doing in the disco that time of night anyway is what I'd like to know.

Mick   Routing out the yobbos who started the bottle fight that the two wee girls got taken the night to hospital from.

Mairtin Well you'd think they'd have something better to do with their time.

Mick Uh-huh. What was Welsh's message, Mairtin?

Mairtin And maybe them two girls deserved a bottling anyways. You don't know the full facts.

Mary Why would poor girls deserve a bottling, sure?

Mairtin Every why. Maybe the piss out of a fella's trainers they took, when all he did was ask them for a danceen, and polite. And then called their bastard brother over to come the hard. Stitches aren't good enough for them sorts of bitches, and well they know. As ugly as them two started out, sure stitches'd be nothing but an improvement, oh aye. (*Pause.*) But as I say, I wasn't there, now, I had a bad leg.

Mick Are you going to make me ask me question again, Mairtin?

Mairtin What question?

Mick What was Welsh's fecking message, for Christ's sake?!

Mairtin (*pause*) Shouting is it, Mick? You're to make a start on this year's exhuming business this coming week. The graveyard shenanigans.

Mary *looks across at* **Mick** *with stern resentment.* **Mick** *avoids her gaze somewhat guiltily.*

Mick This coming week? That's early. In the year, I mean. Although with them burying poor Mag Folan last month there I suppose has hurried things along a little.

Mairtin I don't know if it's hurried things along a little and I don't care if it's hurried things along a little. I'm to help you anyways and twenty quid the week oul Walsh, oul Welsh is to be giving me.

Mick You're to help me?

Mairtin Oul Welsh said. Aye. Twenty quid the week.

How much do you get the week, Mick?

Mick   I get enough the week, and what matter is it to you?

Mairtin   No matter at all, now. Only wondering, I was.

Mick   Well don't be wondering.

Mairtin   Sure, you're the experienced man, anyways. If it's a hundred or if it's more than a hundred, you deserve it, for you're the experienced man. (*Pause.*) Is it more than a hundred, Mick, now?

Mick   This ladeen.

Mairtin   Sure I'm only asking, sure.

Mick   Well that's what you do best is ask eejit questions.

Mairtin   Oh, eejit questions, is it?

Mick   It is.

Mairtin   Ah ... ah ... hmm.

Mary   It's more than you, Mairtin, has questions that that man will not answer.

Mick   Oh, now you're starting with your oul woman bull.

Mairtin   What kind of questions, Mary beag?

Mary   Questions about where did he put our Padraig when he dug him up is the kind of question, and where did he put our Bridgit when he dug her up is the kind of question, and where did he put my poor ma and da when he dug them up is the biggest question!

Mairtin   Where *did* you put all Mary's relations, Mick then, now? The oul bones and the whatnot.

Mary   He won't let on.

Mick   Will I not let on?

Mary   Let on so.

Mairtin   Aye, let on so.

Mick Oh, now you're chipping in.

Mairtin I *am* chipping in. What did you do with them?

Mick What did I do with them, is it?

Mairtin It is. For the hundredth fecking time it is.

Mick Oh, for the hundredth fecking time, is it? I'll tell you what I did with them. I hit them with a hammer until they were dust and I pegged them be the bucketload into the slurry.

Mary *is aghast.* **Mairtin** *bursts out laughing loudly.*

Mairtin (*laughing*) Is that true, now?

Mick Oh, maybe it's true now, and maybe it isn't at all.

Mairtin You hit them with a hammer and you pegged them in the slurry? Can I do that, now, Mick?

Mick No, you can't do that.

Mairtin Ah, you don't hammer no corpses at all. Probably seal them up and put them somewhere is all you do. Put them in the lake or somewhere, when no beggar's about.

Mick Maybe it's in the lake I put them, aye. This is the expert.

Mary *has been keeping* **Mick** *in a stern, fixed stare all the while.*

Mary Mick Dowd!

Mick Maryjohnny!

Mary I am going to ask you one question! And I want the truth!

Mick Ask away for yourself!

Mary Is that right what you said that you hammer the bones to nothing and you throw them in the slurry?

Mick What I do with the bones, both the priest and the guards have swore me to secrecy and bound by them I am . . .

Mairtin   Oh ho.

Mary (*standing*)   Michael Dowd, if you do not answer, bound or not bound, I shall leave this devil-taken house and never darken its . . . !

Mick   Bound I am by the priest and the guards . . .

Mary   Michael Dowd, if you do not answer . . .

Mick   I neither hammer the bones nor throw them in the slurry, Mary. Sure what do you take me for?

Mairtin   I knew well, sure . . .

Mary   So what is it you do with them so, if it isn't hammer?

Mick (*pause*)   I seal them in a bag and let them sink to the bottom of the lake and a string of prayers I say over them as I'm doing so.

Mairtin   I told you, now, it was the fecking lake, or the lake rather. Didn't I tell you now that that's what it was, that he sealed them in a bag and he pegged them in the lake?

Mick   I didn't say I pegged them. I said I gently *eased* them.

Mairtin   Oh aye, you eased them in there, like. And said a couple of prayers over them, aye.

Mick   And said a couple of prayers over them.

Mairtin   To make it official, like.

Mary   Is that the truth, Mick Dowd?

Mick   That's the truth, Mary beag.

Mary   I shall sit and finish that sup with you, so.

Mick   Good on you, Mary.

Mary *sits back down.* **Mick** *refills her glass.*

Mairtin (*eyeing the poteen*) After seven years, sure, it's only a poor straggle of two or three bones they are anyway, I'm sure, and nothing to hammer at all.

Mick The expert on the matter now we're listening to.

Mairtin It's nothing to do with expert. Pure oul common sense is all it has to do with.

Mick Now you're explaining it to me.

Mairtin There's been a cow in our field dead four or five years . . .

Mick I know there has. And that's the best cow you have.

Mairtin No, no, now. Not the best cow we have. It wasn't even our cow at all. Didn't it just wander into our fields one day and fall over dead?

Mick Aye. The smell knocked it.

Mairtin And isn't it now just the . . . 'The smell knocked it.' Feck you. The smell of this house? Eh? 'The smell knocked it'? I'll tell you, boy, eh? (*Pause.*) What was it I was saying, now? You've made me forget . . .

Mick 'Isn't it now just the something . . .'

Mairtin Isn't it now just the skull and a couple of bones left on it, the cow, and no hide nor hair other than that? So wouldn't the body of a person be even less than that, it being rotting in the ground?

Mick You have a point there. Except the body of a person your family wouldn't have been picking at for yere dinners the last five years.

Mairtin Picking at it for our dinners, is it? We do have a sight better dinners in our house than you do in this fecking house anyways! I'll tell you that now! Poteen breakfasts and poteen suppers is all I ever see consumed in this house!

Mick True enough for yourself.

Mairtin   Eh? Insulting our mam's dinners, when all it was was explaining about the cow in our field and the bones was all I was doing. Explaining, so as to help you.

Mick   You're right there, now, Mairtin. I wasn't thinking.

Mairtin   Right? I know I'm right.

Mick   And if I insulted you or your mam or your mam's dinners by casting aspersions you pick the meat off cows five years dead and can't tell the differ, then I take it all back and I apologise.

Mairtin (*confused*)   Eh? Uh-huh? Well, okay. Good.

Mick *pours himself another drink.*

Mairtin   And just to show there's no hard feelings, the tiniest of sips, now, let me take a taste of, Mick. This much, even.

Mick   That much, is it?

Mairtin   That's all. To show there's no hard feelings, now.

Mick   To show there's no hard feelings, aye.

He pours a small amount of poteen out onto his fingers and tosses it at **Mairtin** *as if it's holy water. It hits* **Mairtin** *in the eyes.*

Bless yourself, now, Mairtin.

Mary *laughs slightly.* **Mick** *sits back down.* **Mairtin** *rubs his eyes angrily.*

Mairtin   Got me in the eye, that did!

Mick   Sure that's where I was aiming. I'll bet it stung too.

Mairtin   It *did* sting too, you stinking fecker you. (**Mary** *tuts.*) Tut at me, you? Tut at him would be more in your line when he throws poteen in me eyes, near blinds me.

Mary   You'll know now not again to be disruptive in choir, Mairtin beag.

Mairtin   Choir?! What has fecking choir to do with

anything?! He insults me mam's cooking, throws poteen in me eyes.

Mick   Sure it was only a drop, sure. Would I be wasting good poteen on your eyes?

Mairtin (*to* **Mary**)   Has it gone red, Gran?

Mary   A bit red, Mairtin . . .

Mick   'Gone red.' Jeez, you always was a wussy oul pussy, Mairtin, and nothing but a wussy oul pussy.

Mairtin   A wussy oul pussy, is it?

Mick   It is.

Mairtin   Well maybe I am at that, and maybe I know something that you don't know too.

Mick   What do you know? Skitter you know, Mairtin beag.

Mairtin   Maybe I know which corner of the cemetery it is we're to be digging this week.

Mick   What do I care which corner of the cemetery?

Mairtin   Oh, maybe you don't, now. Only that it's the south side, by the gable.

Mick *nods, somewhat disturbed.*

Mick   Are they all more than seven years down, then, at the gable. They are, I suppose.

Mairtin   They are. Seven years and more! (*To* **Mary**.) See? He doesn't like it when it starts to get closer to home. That's when he doesn't like it.

Mary   What do you mean, 'closer to home'?

Mairtin   Isn't it his missus buried down there by the gable? How closer to home can you get?

Mary   Is Oona buried at the gable, Mick, now?

Mick   She is.

Mary   Oh, God love you . . .

Mairtin   That'll be an interesting job anyways. It isn't many's the man gets paid for digging up the bones of his own dead wife.

Mick   Oona left those bones a long time ago, and that's the only thing that they are now, is bones.

Mary (*quietly*)   You can't go digging up Oona, Mick. That's not right. Leave Oona to somebody else, now.

Mick   To who? To him? He'd probably crack her head in two, so he would.

Mairtin   Oh. Crack her head in two, is it?

Mick   It is.

Mairtin   I heard that's already been done.

Mick (*pause. Standing, advancing*)   What did you hear?

Mairtin   Just a thing or two, now, and don't you be fecking advancing on me, because saying nothing I was, only some people say things and I pay no mind at all until some other people start shouting the odds and calling me names and pegging poteen in me eyes . . .

Mick   What names did I call you?

Mary (*pause. Quietly*)   A wussy oul pussy . . .

Mairtin   A wussy oul pussy you called me. And if people start doing that then I'll have to be pegging something back at them, and it isn't a smatter of poteen it'll be, it'll be aspersions. And if the aspersions are true or not I don't know, and I don't care. I only threw them out because it was you who started the whole shebang in the first place.

Mick   What *are* the aspersions anyways?

Mairtin   Just general ones.

Mick   The only aspersions that could be cast are the ones I've already admitted to, and the ones I've already served me time over. That I had had a drink taken, and a good drink, and that she had no seat-belt on her, and that was the end of it. No other aspersions could there be.

Mairtin   Well, sure, that was the aspersion I was saying anyways, the drink-driving aspersion. What aspersion did you think I was saying?

Mick (*pause*)   That was the aspersion you was saying?

Mairtin   Aye. (*Pause.*)   What was . . .

Mick   Well even that aspersion is seven years past, yet straight to me face you go casting your fecking . . .

Mairtin   Well isn't that better than the most of them round here? Will smile at you 'til you're a mile away before they start talking behind your back. One thing about me, anyways. I'm honest.

Mick (*to* **Mary**)   Do people be talking behind my bank?

Mary   They do not. He's a wee get with nothing but cheek.

Mairtin   A wee get is it? And they don't be talking behind his back? Uh-huh. It must be some other fella who drove his wife into a wall, so, they must be talking about. I must be mistaken. I often am.

Mick (*quietly*)   Leave this house, Mairtin Hanlon.

Mairtin   I *will* leave this house, the welcome I got here, after coming all this way with the message from oul Welsh, Walsh, Welsh. Not only no welcome but a spray of poteen that almost took me eyes out as a thank you, not to mention the names called, and the insulted mam's dinners. Uh-huh. (*Exits. Re-enters.*) Um . . . will they have a spade at the church I can use, Mick, for I have no spade?

Mary   Your father has a rake of spades, sure.

Mairtin   My father has no rake of spades. He has a rake of rakes. He has no spade. The only spade he has are the handles of two spades, and nothing but the handles, which you couldn't call a spade at all. Rakes he has a stack of, and I don't know why, because there is no call for them. There is always more call for a spade than a rake. In my opinion.

Mick   They'll have a spade at the church.

Mairtin   Will they have a spade at the church? Except they'll need two spades. One for the both of us . . .

Mick   They'll have two spades.

Mairtin   Are you positive, now? I don't want to be walking all that way . . .

Mick   Mairtin, will you ever feck off home for yourself?!

Mairtin   Feck off home, is it? I'll feck off home, all right. I don't have to be asked twice.

Mick   No, fecking five times you have to be asked!

Mairtin (*exiting*)   Uh-huh, I don't have to be asked twice.

Mary (*pause*)   The tongue on that one.

Pause. They drink their poteen a while, staring into the fire.

Mick   Is it true, Mary?

Mary   Is what true, Mick?

Mick   The talking behind my back.

Mary   There is no talking behind your back. He's a wee eejit, or if not an eejit then a blackguard, and we both know the truth of that.

Mick   Aye.

Mary   Sure the time he put the werewolf comic in with Mrs Dunphy, and hadn't they almost nailed the lid on her before we noticed?

Mick   Aye.

Mary   If that had gone ahead, just think. (*Pause.*) The boy's a wee blackguard and nothing else, and even though he's me own grandson I'll admit it, he's a rotten blackguard with nothing but cheek, so don't you even be thinking about it.

Mick   Aye. (*Pause.*) Aye, I suppose you're right.

Mary   I *am* right, sure.

Mick   Aye.

Mary   Right? There's no question, right.

Mick   There's not, I suppose. No. (*Pause.*) No. (*Pause.*) And there's been no other aspersions cast with my name on them, other than those . . .

Mary   There's been no other aspersions, Mick. (*Pause.*) None at all, sure. (*Pause.*) Sure we all know the type of man you are, Mick Dowd.

Mick *looks across at her.*

Mick   Aye . . . Is right.

Mary *smiles at him slightly. They both stare at the fire again. Curtain.*

Scene Two

A rocky cemetery at night, lit somewhat eerily by a few lamps dotted about. Two graves with gravestones atop a slight incline in the centre. At the start of the scene, the grave on the right is in the process of being dug up by **Mick**, *standing down inside it to waist height, shoveling the dirt out.* **Mairtin** *lays his shovel down, sits against the right-hand gravestone behind him, and lights a cigarette.*

Mairtin   I'm taking a cigarette break.

Mick   A break from what, sure? You've done no work.

Mairtin   I've done my biteen.

Mick   A bit of shite you've done.

Mairtin   I have a blister too, and I didn't even mention it.

Mick   You've mentioned it now.

Mairtin   For fear I'd be accused of complaining. (*Pause. Looking at the next-door grave.*) When will we be starting on your missus's patch anyways? Going around in circles to avoid it we seem to be.

Mick   We go in order. We don't skip two ahead.

Mairtin   Skip? That's all we've been doing is skipping, if you're asking my opinion. (*Pause.*) I'll make a start on your missus's grave.

Mick   Will you, now?

Mairtin   I may.

Mairtin *takes his shovel and idles past* **Mick** *to Oona's grave.* **Mick** *stops work and looks at him threateningly.* **Mairtin** *taps the soil with his foot, then raises his shovel as if about to start digging.*

Mick   One grain of that soil you touch, Mairtin Hanlon, it is *in* that grave you will be, not on it.

Mairtin *smiles, lays his shovel aside, and leans against the gravestone behind him.*

Mairtin   Is it murder you're threatening now, Mick, and in earshot of your missus too?

Mick   It isn't murder, because self-defence it would be, as protection from your wittering on like a fecking oul hen. I would be doing the community a service.

Mairtin   The community a service? I heard you already did the community a service.

Mick   What service?

Mairtin   The community service you did, when they let you out of jail early.

Mick   Now you're starting again.

Mick *returns to his digging.*

Mairtin I'm just saying, like.

Mick Now you're trying to come the clever.

Mairtin Well, as I say to Sheila Fahey, it isn't too hard I have to try to come the clever, because I *am* clever.

Mick Clever, is it? And is it ten times you've failed the Leaving Certificate now, or is it eleven times?

Mairtin It's one time.

Mick Oh, is it one time, now?

Mairtin The other time it coincided with me wrongful expulsion.

Mick Your wrongful expulsion? Uh-huh. The cat you cooked alive in biology?

Mairtin · It wasn't me at all, now, Mick, and they knew full well it wasn't me, and didn't they have to reinstate me on the spot when Blind Billy Pender came out and confessed, with not a word of apology from them.

Mick Poor backward Blind Billy Pender, aye, whom you didn't influence in his confession at all.

Mairtin And it was a hamster anyways, if you would like to get your facts right.

Mick I don't need help from the likes of you to get me facts right.

Mairtin Oh aye.

Mick I'll tell you that anyways.

Mairtin (*pause*) Let's get a start on your missus's grave, Mick.

Mick (*pause*) We'll get a start when we've finished this one. And when the guard arrives.

Mairtin When the guard arrives? Oh. Is there a law, so, you can't dig up your wife unless you have the polis there?

Mick   Something of the like. Or, anyways, the guard had a word, said I'd best make sure he was there before we made a start. To save tongues wagging anyways.

Mairtin   What would tongues be wagging for?

Mick   I don't know. Just for the sake of it.

Sound of **Mick***'s shovel hitting the rotten wood at the bottom of the grave.*

Mairtin   Are you through to him?

Mick   Pass me the sack down.

Mairtin *jumps up from where he is and looks down into the grave. Sound of* **Mick** *jimmying rotten wood apart with his shovel. He picks the bits of wood up and throws them out of the grave.*
Mairtin *moves around a little to get a better view of the corpse.*

Mairtin   Ay yi yi, look at that one. Who is he? (*Glances behind.*) Daniel Faragher. Never heard of him.

Mick   I knew him to say hello to.

Mairtin   Would you recognise him?

Mick *looks at* **Mairtin** *as if he's stupid.*

Mairtin   Not from his bare skull, no, of course. Although he still has a lock of hair there, now. He looks like a big dolly.

Mick   A what?

Mairtin   A big dolly. Like girls do play with.

Mick   The girls won't be playing with this dolly.

Mairtin   I know that, sure. I'm only saying. How old would he be, then?

Mick   He would be . . .

Mairtin   No, let me guess, now.

Mick   Guess ahead.

Mairtin   A pound if I guess right.

Mick   And a pound to me if you guess wrong.

Mairtin   Okay. (*Glances at headstone and calculates.*) He was, I'd say . . . about sixty-seven now.

Mick   Wrong. *Seventy*-seven he was. You owe me a pound.

Mairtin *looks back at the headstone again, recalculates on his fingers, and realises his mistake.*

Mairtin   Ah feck.

Mick   And pass me the sack, for the fiftieth time.

Mairtin *goes off mumbling behind the headstones.*

Mairtin   I'll pass you the fecking sack . . .

. . . and returns with a large, dirty black cloth sack half-full of the bones and skulls of two corpses. **Mairtin** *passes it to* **Mick**.

Pass your skull to me, Mick. Just to compare, now.

Mick *tosses* **Mairtin** *the skull with the lock of hair on it, then starts placing the bones from the grave into the sack, keeping a quiet eye on* **Mairtin** *all the while as he idles around with the skulls, placing them against his chest as if they're breasts at one point, kissing them together at another.*

Mairtin   Sure skulls are great oul things. It's hard to believe you have one of these on the inside of your head.

Mick   It's hard to believe *you* have one of them anyways, and the brain to go with it.

Mairtin   I have no brain, is it? I have a brain too, and a big brain.

Mick   Kissing skulls together. Like an oul schoolgirl.

Mairtin (*pause*)   When do oul schoolgirls kiss skulls together, sure?

Mick (*pause*)   I'm just saying, like.

Mairtin   Oul schoolgirls can't get ahold of skulls at all.

He pokes a finger in the skulls' eye sockets.

You can stick your fingers right in their eyes.

Mick (*pause. Confused*)   Oul schoolgirls' eyes, now?

Mairtin   Skulls' eyes, now! Why would you be sticking your fingers in schoolgirls' eyes?

Mick   I don't know, now.

Mairtin *hands the skulls back to* **Mick** *who places them in the sack, then quietly crouches down and looks into the grave.*

Mairtin   Hey, Mick!

Mick   What?

Mairtin   Where does your thing go?

Mick   Eh?

Mairtin   Where does your thing go? When you die, I mean. None of them have had their things at all. And I've looked.

Mick   I know well you've looked. And the women's too! I think that's why you came on this job, to have a good look. You don't see many living ones.

Mairtin   I see my share.

Mick   Of willies, now, Mairtin?

Mairtin   Of the other, and you know well!

Mick   Do you really not know where they go? Have you never been told?

Mairtin   No.

Mick   They don't tell you in religious studies?

Mairtin   No. I do skip a lot of religious studies. It's just a lot of stuff about Jesus.

Mick   That's the reason you don't know, so. Isn't it illegal in the Catholic faith to bury a body the willy still attached? Isn't it a sin in the eyes of the Lord?

Mairtin   (*incredulous*)   No . . .

Mick Don't they snip them off in the coffin and sell them to tinkers as dog food.

Mairtin (*horrified*) They do not!

Mick And during the famine, didn't the tinkers stop feeding them to their dogs at all and start sampling the merchandise themselves?

Mairtin They did not, now, Mick . . .

Mick You would see them riding along with them, munching ahead.

Mairtin No . . .

Mick That's the trouble with young people today, is they don't know the first thing about Irish history.

Mick *smiles to himself.* **Mairtin**, *sickened, sees this and begins to doubt.*

Mairtin That isn't true.

Mick As true as I'm standing here.

Mairtin I'll go up and ask oul Walsh, Welsh, at the church so. He'd be the man to know.

Mick Go ahead, so.

Mairtin Eh?

Mick Go on ahead and ask for yourself.

Mairtin I *will* go on ahead and ask.

Mick Go so.

Mairtin (*pause*) And ask do they cut the willies off and give them to tinkers?

Mick Aye.

Mairtin (*pause*) I'll go so.

Mick So go.

Mairtin I'm going. I don't need you to tell me to be going.

Mairtin *slowly idles off stage left.* **Mick** *smiles to himself when he's gone, then gets out of the grave he's in, having finished collecting its bones, lifts the sack out with him and puts it to one side. He idles over stage left to his wife's grave and looks down at it a while, hands in pockets. Enter the guard,* **Thomas Hanlon**, *stage right, in full uniform, sucking on, at intervals throughout, a cigarette and an asthma inhaler.*

Thomas You haven't started?

Mick I haven't started.

Thomas What are you doing so?

Mick I'm just looking at it.

Thomas Oh aye. No harm. I had some trouble out at the Riordan's Hall is why I'm late. Two women fighting and one man.

Mick Was the two women fighting the man or who was fighting who?

Thomas The two women was fighting among themselves and getting on fine when this oul fella butted in saying 'It's not right women fighting, break it up', and didn't the two of them deck him and take it in turns treading on him?

Mick Good enough for him. What business was it of his them fighting. I like a good fight between women.

Thomas The same as that, I like a good fight between women, although I couldn't say that while on duty, like. We arrested the lot of them anyways. The oul fella couldn't believe it. Went crying he did. Crying and wouldn't stop crying. And Johnny Doyle said 'I'll give you a batter too if you don't stop', but even then he wouldn't stop.

Mick Did he give him a batter so?

Thomas Ah no, now. There's no call to batter oul fellas, even if they're crying.

Mick There's not I suppose.

Thomas Ah no. Sure we'll be oul fellas too someday.

Mick (*pause*) I'll get a start on this, so.

Thomas Go ahead for yourself, aye.

Mick *starts digging up his wife's grave.* **Thomas** *sits against the right-hand headstone and looks inside the black sack, grimacing a little.*

Thomas Awful morbid work this is, Mick.

Mick It's work to be done.

Thomas Awful ghoulish though.

Mick Work to be done it is. Isn't the space needed?

Thomas I'm certain there are other ways. Encouraging cremation is what the church should be. Not all this.

Mick Who around here would go for cremation? No one.

Thomas It's got to be better than this every year.

Mick Get onto them so. (*Pause.*) Don't you come across more morbid things than this in your work every day? People only minutes dead you come across, neverminding seven years.

Thomas When do I come across people only minutes dead?

Mick Do you not? Oh. I thought the way you do talk about it, just like *Hill Street Blues* your job is. Bodies flying about everywhere.

Thomas I would *like* there to be bodies flying about everywhere, but there never is.

Mick Go ahead up north so. You'll be well away. Hang about a bookies or somewhere.

Thomas Ah there's no detective work in that oul bullshit. Detective work I'm talking about. You know, like *Quincy*.

Mick Oh, like *Quincy*. (*Pause.*) Have you never seen a dead body, so? A just dead body?

Thomas The only body I've ever seen was a fella in a block of flats the road to Shannon. The fattest bastard you've ever seen in your life. Tits like this. Sitting, no clothes, in his armchair. No clothes, now. Television still on. A heart attack, the doctor said. All well and good. He knows more than me. But I had meself a look in that fat man's fridge, now. A mighty fridge it was, six feet high. What was in there? A pot of jam and a lettuce. Eh? And nothing else. A pot of jam and a lettuce in the fridge of the fattest man you've ever seen in your life. Nothing suspicious in that? I pointed it out in my report to them, and they just laughed at me. And watching television stark naked too? Nothing suspicious in that?

Mick (*pause*) What time of year was it?

Thomas What time of year? I don't know . . .

Mick If it was the height of summer, and he wasn't expecting any visitors, it might very well explain the stark naked.

Thomas (*pause*) It might explain the stark naked, aye. It might not explain the complete absence of food in his six-foot fridge! Eh?

Mick You have a point.

Thomas I have a point, aye. I know I have a point. The amount of food a fat fella eats? He won't get far on a lettuce and a pot of jam! Just laughed at me they did. (*Pause.*) Where's the young shite anyways?

Mick Gone up to the church. I told him to ask the priest is it right the Church hands out the willies of the dead to passing tinker children to play with.

Thomas And he hasn't gone?

Mick He has gone.

Thomas Oh he's as thick as five thick fellas, that fecker. What do they teach them in school now anyways?

Mick I don't know what they teach them. Cooking cats they teach them.

Thomas   Cooking cats, aye. No. A hamster it was.

Mick   It's the same difference, sure.

Thomas   Pardon me?

Mick   It's the same difference, I said.

Thomas   It's not the same difference at all, sure. A cat is one thing. A hamster is another.

Mick   Is it worth the argue, now?

Thomas   I'm just saying, like. (*Pause.*) A fact is a fact, like. It's the same in detective work. No matter how small a detail may appear to be, you can't go lumping it with a bunch of other details like it's all the same thing. So you can't go lumping cats and hamsters together either. Things like that are the difference between solving and not solving an entire case, sure.

Mick   Oh aye, aye, they are, I suppose.

Mick *returns to his digging.*

Thomas   They are. They certainly are. Oh aye. (*Pause.*) How far are you down?

Mick   I'm down a good way. Funny, this soil's easy digging . . .

Mairtin *returns, angry, rubbing his cheek.*

Mairtin   A back-fecking-hander the fecker gave me, you fecking bastard ya!

Mick *and* **Thomas** *laugh.*

Mairtin   What the feck are yous laughing for, you feckers you?

Thomas   Stop your cursing now, Mairtin. Not in the graveyard. Against God so it is.

Mairtin   Against God, is it?

Thomas   It is.

Mairtin   Feck God so! And his mother too!

Both **Mick** *and* **Thomas** *stop to chastise* **Mairtin**, **Thomas** *standing.*

Mick   Hey...!!

Thomas   Now, Mairtin, I'm liable to give you a batter meself if you go on like that, and a better batter it will be than the one you got from that biteen of a priest.

Mairtin   Ah, go to blazes with you.

Thomas   A bloody better batter it will be.

Mairtin   Of course. Aren't the polis the experts at battering gasurs anyway? Don't you get a bonus for it?

Mick *continues digging.*

Thomas   What gasurs do I ever batter?

Mairtin   Ray Dooley for a start-off, or if not you then your bastarding cohorts.

Thomas   What about Ray Dooley?

Mairtin   Didn't he end up the County Hospital ten minutes after you arrested him?

Thomas   He did, the pisshead, a broken toe. Kicking the cell door in and forgetting he had no shoes on him.

Mairtin   Aye, that's what *you* say. That's what *you* say.

Thomas *(pause)*   Don't be cursing God in a graveyard, anyway, is what the crux of the matter is.

Mairtin   Aye, and don't be invading people's human rights is what the other crux of the matter is. The guards are there to serve the people, not the other way round, if you'd like to know.

Thomas   You've been paying attention in Sociology class anyways, Mairtin.

Mairtin I have.

Thomas That's a good thing. Is it still Miss Byrne with the mini-skirts teaches that?

Mairtin I'm not bandying around pleasantries with the likes of you!

Mick Get back to fecking work, so, and start filling that one in.

Mairtin *tuts and goes to the right-hand grave with his shovel. He starts tipping the dirt back into it.*

Mairtin (*to* **Thomas**) I see you say nothing to him when he says 'feck' in the graveyard. Is it only kids, so you go shouting the odds with?

Thomas It is, aye. Only kids.

Mairtin I know well it is.

Thomas I do like to specialise.

Mairtin I know you do. (*Pause. Mumbling.*) Specialise me black arsehole.

As **Mairtin** *continues shovelling dirt at the grave's edge,* **Thomas** *quietly walks up behind him and shoves him down into it.* **Mairtin** *yelps.* **Mick** *and* **Thomas** *laugh, kicking dirt down onto him.* **Mairtin** *quickly clambers up from the rotten coffin underfoot.*

Mairtin You're a fecking fecker, Thomas. And you're nothing else.

Thomas (*laughing*) Haven't I told you, now, about your language?

Mairtin I'm going the feck home.

Thomas You're not going the feck home either. I've told dad to give you a batter himself if you're home before daybreak. So there you are.

Mairtin You're always ganging up on me, the fecking two of ye.

Thomas   Ah, the babby's going crying now. Go on and help Mick, whiny, or I'll tell oul Welsh to be docking your wages on you.

Mairtin (*pause*)   Do you need help with the digging there, Mick?

Mick   No. Go on ahead with your filling in that one.

Mairtin *does so.* **Thomas** *lights a cigarette.*

Thomas (*pause*)   Aren't you getting nervous there now, Mick? I'd be nervous, seeing me wife again after such a time.

Mick   What's to be nervous for?

Mairtin   Aye, what's to be nervous for?

Thomas   Nothing at all, now.

Mick   Nothing at all is right.

Thomas   Aye, now. Only I thought you might have some things on your mind might be making you nervous seeing your missus again.

Mick   What kind of things on me mind?

Mairtin   Aye, what kind of things on his mind?

Thomas   I don't know, now. I have no idea at all. Just things on your mind, like.

Mick   I have no things on me mind.

Thomas   Good-oh. I was just saying, like.

Mick   What things are you saying I have on me mind?

Thomas   No things at all, sure. None at all. Just conversing we are.

Mick   Conversing me arse. Do you have something to say to me?

Thomas   No, no, now . . .

Mick   Because if you do, go ahead and spit it out. Is it me drink-driving you're saying?

Thomas   I was saying nothing, now, Mick.

Mick   Casting aspersions on me . . . ?

Thomas   I was casting no aspersions at all . . .

Mick   The family of eejits and blackguards you come from?

Mairtin (*pause*)   Who's an eejit and a blackguard? Is it me he's talking about, Thomas?

Thomas   It is, aye.

Mairtin (*pause*)   How do you know it's me he's talking about? It could've been you or dad or anybody he was talking about.

Thomas   Who were you talking about, Mick?

Mick   Him.

Thomas (*to* **Mairtin**)   See?

Mairtin   Ya feck!

Thomas   Now, Mick, you've insulted poor wee Mairtin there, you've insulted family, such as it is, so now I have to go and say something insulting back to you. That is the way that these things operate.

Mick   You're the one who started with the insults.

Thomas   No, Mick, no. I have to take you up on that. You're the one who started with the insults. I was the one who started with the vague insinuations.

Mick   It's the self-same thing.

Thomas   Pardon me?

Mick   It's the self-same thing, I said.

Thomas   It's not the self-same thing at all, and if you knew anything about the law then you'd know it's not the self-same thing. So now I have to turn me vague insinuations into something more of an insult, so then we'll all be quits . . .

Mairtin (*to* **Mick**)   Your ma was a queer and your da was a queer and how they came up with you is a mystery of the Universe!

Both **Mick** *and* **Thomas** *stare blankly at* **Mairtin** *for a few moments, who looks away, embarrassed. Pause.*

Thomas   No, what I was going to say was . . . some insinuation along the lines of . . . not that I'm making any accusations, mind . . . but maybe your wife's head injuries all those years ago weren't especially conducive to only having been in a car crash at all, and maybe . . .

Mick (*angrily*)   All that came out at the time, Thomas Hanlon, and didn't the inquest shoot every word of it down!

Thomas   Y'know, maybe she was already dead *before* you drove her into the wall, that kind of insinuation, like. But nothing harsher than that am I saying,

Mick   Take all of that back, Thomas Hanlon!

Thomas   I'm only suggesting, now, like.

Mick   Take every word of it back, because if you make me get up out of this grave, now, polis or not . . .

Thomas   You take eejit and blackguard back, so, and I'll be pleased to take it back.

Mick   You take your things back first.

Thomas   No, now. You said your things first, so it's only fair you take them back first too.

Mick   There was no call for any of this.

Thomas   I agree with you, like.

Mick   For any of these insults. (*Pause.*) I take eejit and blackguard back.

Thomas   I take wife-butcherer back, so.

Mairtin *laughs loudly, half in surprise, half in pride, as* **Mick** *and* **Thomas** *stare at each other.*

Mairtin Is that all true?

Mick A pure drink-driving it was, Thomas, and you know full well it was.

Thomas I *do* know full well it was, and I've taken me accusations back without reservation.

Mairtin Is it true, Thomas?

Thomas Of course it's not true, Mairtin. Haven't I just said? I made up every word of it.

Mairtin (*confused*) I thought you were saying it was true.

Thomas Not at all. A pure drink-driving is all it was, just like Mick says.

Mick *and* **Thomas** *stare at each other a few seconds more, then* **Mick** *returns to his digging.*

Mairtin Oh-h. I'm disappointed so.

Thomas Why are you disappointed, babby?

Mairtin There you got me hoping I was working with a fella up and slaughtered his wife with an axe or something, when all it was was an oul cheap-ass drink-driving. Aren't they ten-a-penny? Wouldn't it be hard to find somebody round here who *hasn't* killed somebody drink-driving? Or if not a somebody then a heifer, or at least a dog. Didn't oul Marcus Rigby kill twins with his tractor, and him over seventy?

Thomas No, he did not.

Mairtin Did he not? Who was it killed twins with his tractor so? It was someone.

Thomas No. That was just something I told you when you was twelve to mind you kept out of the road with your bicycle when you saw a tractor coming.

Mairtin (*pause*) There was no twins at all?

Thomas If you had any sense you'd have known when did ever twins live around here?

Mairtin   Twins come over from America I was thinking, to see where *The Quiet Man* was filmed and got lost.

Thomas   You was thinking wrong, so. I only said twins to get you thinking if a tractor killed two gasurs it'd be twice as likely a tractor'd kill you, there only being one of you.

Mairtin (*angrily*)   So all those years I drove me bicycle through hedgerows and banks of skitter and all on account of them poor mangled twins I had on me mind, and it was all for nothing?!

Thomas (*laughing*)   It was, indeed.

Mairtin   You're a bastard of a bastard of a bastard of a feck, Thomas Hanlon!

Thomas   You're still alive anyways, is the main thing. Do you know how many boys the age of eight died falling into slurry tanks the last year in Ireland alone?

Mairtin   I don't! And I don't fecking care!

Thomas   Fourteen. Fourteen of the poor gasurs.

Mairtin   Good! And let them die!

Thomas   And drowning in slurry, Mairtin beag, isn't the nicest way to go out of this world. I'll tell you that for yourself.

Mairtin   Feck drowning in slurry, and feck their mothers too . . . !

Mick (*interrupting*)   That's not true, now, is it, Thomas? The fourteen gasurs drowning in the slurry?

Thomas   It *is* true, aye. (*Pause.*) Not altogether, mind . . .

Mick   No.

Thomas   Not all in the one tank, now. Separately.

Mick   Separately. In different parts of the country, like, and at different times.

Thomas Aye. From the Central Office of Statistics this is. They have good statistics they do. More kids die in slurry tanks than die in combine harvesters. Only seven died in combine harvesters.

Mick Of course. Because more people have slurry tanks than have combine harvesters.

Thomas That's true enough.

Mick It's only rich people have combine harvesters. And their kids are less thick anyways.

Thomas Is right.

Mick To go climbing in slurry you have to be thick.

Thomas You do.

Mairtin (*angrily*) It wasn't climbing in slurry this conversation was at all! This conversation was the lie about the dead twins!

As he speaks, **Thomas** *pushes* **Mairtin** *over into the grave again and kicks dirt at him.*

Thomas Ah, shut your creeping bollocks about the dead twins, ya fecking oul shite-arse ya, and you're nothing else.

Mairtin Kick dirt at me, is it?! And . . . and call me an oul shite-arse, is it?!

Thomas It is. You observed well.

Mairtin We'll see about that so, you fecker . . .

Thomas Oh aye, now. The babby's angry . . .

Mairtin *starts clambering up out of the side of the grave to get at* **Thomas**, *who takes his truncheon out in readiness. Just as* **Mairtin** *gets to his feet, the sound of* **Mick**'s *shovel splintering the rotten coffin lid under his feet is heard.*

Mick I'm through to it.

Mairtin *and* **Thomas** *stare at each other a moment, then forget their fight and go and stand over* **Mick** *at the grave.* **Mick** *crouches* *down, so he's almost out of sight, to pull up the rotten boards.*

Thomas Prepare yourself so, Mick, now. She'll be a shock to you.

Mick The boards are . . . funny. The boards are already broke open, or is that just the rot, now?

Mick *throws a couple of bits of rotten board away.*

Thomas Dig some more of that dirt off there, Mick.

Mick *takes his shovel and scrapes some more of the dirt from the coffin. After a few seconds, his scraping starts becoming more frantic.*

Mick What's the . . . ? What's the . . . ?

Thomas Is she . . . ?

Mairtin This is a peculiar business.

Mick *throws the shovel away and ducks down into the grave again, this time desperately scraping the dirt away with his bare hands.*

Mick (*frantic*) Where is she . . . ?! Where is she . . . ?!

Thomas (*quietly*) Is she not . . . ?

Mick (*shouting, voice almost breaking*) She's not there!

His scraping ceases. Pause. He stands back up, dirty and bedraggled, looking down into the grave numbly.

(*Quietly.*) She's not there.

Pause. Blackout.

Scene Three

Night, a day or two later. Set the same as in Scene One. Three skulls and their sets of bones lie on the table in front of **Mairtin** *who stares dumbly down at them, swaying, drunk, blowing bubbles. He has a mallet in one hand and a quarter-empty bottle of poteen in the other, from which he takes disgusted sips every now and then.* **Mick** *can be heard rummaging through a toolbox offstage. He is also drunk.*

Mick (*off*)   There's another one here somewhere I know.

Mairtin   What do you be wanting an oul woody hammer for, Mick, now?

Mick   They do call them mallets.

Mairtin   Ohh. (*Pause.*) Skulls do be more scary on your table than they do be in their coffin. Why? I don't know why. Some reason now.

Mick   Are you getting scared, you wee pup?

Mairtin   I'm not getting scared at all. All right I'm getting a bit scared. You won't be leaving me on me own more long?

Mick   The minute I find this feck I'll be with you. No chance of you helping me look.

Mairtin (*absently*)   No. (*Pause.*) Weren't they terrible heathens whoever pinched your missus on you?

Mick   They were. And if I ever got me hands on the fecks, then we'd see.

Mairtin   What would you do to them, Mick? Would you give them a kick?

Mick   It would be worse than a kick.

Mairtin   Would you peg stones at them?

Mick   Worse than stones it'd be.

Mairtin   Peg . . . biteens'a . . . rocks . . .

Mick   You wouldn't have heard tell of who took her, Mairtin? Not one of your oul mates, I'm thinking?

Mairtin   None of my mates. What would one of my mates be wanting with your oul missus? My mates don't be fooling with dead missuses.

Mick   And can we rule you off the list of suspects too?

Mairtin   I'm on no list of suspects. If I was to be digging up your missus it's good money I'd be wanting for the job, the same as you, cash in hand. Maybe it was a set of tinkers dug her up on you.

Mick   What would tinkers be wanting with her?

Mairtin   I don't know. Maybe they were expecting another praitie blight and felt like something to be munching on ahead of time. Not that there'd be much to munch on with your missus. No willy anyways. As far as I know anyways, I didn't know the woman. I still can't believe that about them willies. That's an awful thing.

Mick   Found the feck!

Mick *enters, a half-empty bottle of poteen in one hand, a mallet in the other, which he shows to* **Mairtin**.

Mairtin   What will we be playing so, Mick? That oul game with the hoops and the sticks they do play in England with the hoops and the sticks and the balls they do play in England, what's it called, with the hoops and the sticks? They do play it in England. It has a 'c'.

Mick   Are you looking in me eyes now, Mairtin?

Mairtin   What eyes?

Mick   *My* eyes.

Mairtin   Aye, your eyes. *Croquet!*

Mick   Did you have anything to do with my wife going missing?

Mairtin   Eh?

Mick   Did you have anything to do with my wife going missing?

Mairtin   No.

Mick *keeps staring at* **Mairtin** *for a long time, as* **Mairtin** *sways slightly but returns the stare.*

Mick   You have looked me in the eyes and I believe you now, Mairtin. I do apologise for even asking you.

Mairtin Good-oh.

Mick *shakes* **Mairtin** *by the hand and walks over to the table.*

Mick Are these skulls still scaring you?

Mairtin I'm less scared now but don't be leaving me on me own again with them. When they get me on me own they do go smiling at me. Especially that one.

Mick Shall we be teaching them a lesson then so?

Mairtin Sure you can't teach skulls lessons. They have no brain to be sticking the . . . lesson . . .

Mick Knowledge?

Mairtin Knowledge. They have no brain to be sticking the lesson through the holes knowledge into.

Mick This is the only lesson skulls be understanding.

He brings the mallet crashing down on the skull nearest to him, shattering it, spraying pieces of it all over the room.

He won't be smiling no more.

Mairtin You've buggered him to skitter!

Mick I have. Not skitter enough.

Mick *starts smashing the skull into even smaller pieces and stamping on the bits that have fallen on the floor.* **Mairtin** *stares at him dumbfounded.*

Mairtin Ease them in the lake you said.

Mick In front of the fat one I said, aye. Batter the shite out of them is nearer the mark. And why not? If it's whispering about me they're going to be through the years, what more should they expect when they wind up in my hands than batter?

Mairtin Nothing more.

Mick Nothing more is right.

Mairtin May I be having a batter, Mick? Ah let me now.

Mick   Why else have I invited you here with a hammer in your hand?

Mairtin   I can? Ohh Jeebies ... Goodbye Daniel Faragher. You've been smiling at me long enough, boy.

Mairtin *takes a little run-up and starts smashing another of the skulls and its bones to pieces. The smashing continues more or less unabated by at least one of the men throughout most of the rest of the scene.*

Mick   That one's Biddy Curran, not Dan Faragher at all.

Mairtin   Biddy Curran, ya currant bun, ya ...

Mick   She was a fat oul bitch.

Mairtin   She's thin enough now, God bless her. And getting more thin.

Mick   The middle one's Dan, and Dan's mine.

Mick *starts smashing the middle skull.*

Mairtin   Ar, you've done two and I've only done one, Mick, ya snatching feck.

Mick   Don't be going crying, Mairtin. And haven't you had half a bottle of poteen off me today if I'm such a snatching' feck?

Mairtin   I have. (*Drinks.*) You're not a snatching feck at all. You're a generous man.

Mick   You can join in with Dan's bones if you like.

Mairtin   I'll be taking a pop at Biddy Curran's pelvis and then I'll see how I'm feeling.

Mick   Good-oh.

Mairtin   Should you not be putting a whatyoucall down to be catching them?

Mick   What matter?

Mairtin Or a thing?

Mick If you'll not be liking my skull-battering ways you can be off with you.

Mairtin Your ways is fine indeed.

Mick I do have a dustpan and brush.

Mairtin I was thinking. Goodbye Biddy Curran or whatever it is your name is. You're all mixed up now anyways, you poor feck you.

Mick Don't be cursing now, Mairtin.

Mairtin I won't be.

Mick Not when you're handling the departed, now.

Mairtin This is more fun than hamster-cooking!

Mick It is. Or if it is I don't know. I've never cooked hamsters.

Mairtin I've only cooked one hamster. It's not all it's cracked up to be. You stick him in alive and he comes out dead. The feck hardly squeals . . . I mean, the fella hardly squeals. If the oven had had a see-through door it would've been more fun, but it didn't, it had an ordinary door. My mistake was not planning ahead. I was egged on. But this is more fun. Is skull-hammering more fun than wife-into-wall-driving, Mick?

Mick Oh Mairtin, you're getting a bit near to the mark there, boy.

Mairtin Oh I am. When I drink I do get awful stupid. I apologise, Mick.

Mick I accept your apology, Mairtin. Seeing as you're drunk as Jaysus.

Mairtin I *am* drunk as Jaysus. But I'll be putting me head in a bucket of water when I get home and I'll be fine then. I do do that of a Saturday night I do, and me dad does never twig I've been drinking.

Mick Be remembering to take your head out of the bucket afterwards is the main thing.

Mairtin I know. Else you'd go drowning.

Mick Is right.

Mairtin *stops hammering abruptly, to launch into his story, and* **Mick** *stops quickly also, to listen.*

Mairtin Did my brother ever tell you the drunk out in Salthill, lay down on the floor to sleep, and where was his head resting? His head was resting in a potty of wee. Drowned he did! On wee! Eh?

Mick On wee, was it?

Mairtin Drowned on wee. What a way to go, eh?

Mick Was it his own wee?

Slight pause.

Mairtin I don't know if it was his own wee or not. And I don't care. He drowned on wee is all I'm saying.

Mick No, now. A fact like that is very important, now. Your brother would be the first to agree.

Mairtin (*pause*) Now that I think of it, I think my brother *did* want to launch an investigation into the matter, but they wouldn't let him. But I don't know if it was whose wee it was was what aroused his suspicions or not. Sure, a pig that smelt would arouse that bastard's suspicions. Thinks he's Starsky and Hutch. (*Pause.*) I, for one, would rather drown on me own wee than on anybody else's. Though I'd rather not drown on wee at all!

Mick I had three uncles drowned on sick.

Mairtin (*pause*) But, sure, drowned on sick is nothing to go shouting about. Doesn't everybody drown on sick?

Mick Three uncles now, I'm saying.

Mairtin Three uncles or no. Drowned on sick is ten-a-penny now, Mick. A million have drowned on sick. Oul

black fella. Jimi Hendrix. Drowned on wee I'm talking
about. Drowned on wee you have to go out of your way.
Drowned on sick you don't. And of course. Sick is there in
your gob already. Wee is nowhere near.

Mick If it's drunk you are and you go to bed and you
fear you may be sick, this is what you should do . . .

He lays down flat on his belly on the floor, his face to one side.

Lay down flat on your belly or on your side, your face
turned to the side of the pillow. Or throw the pillow away
completely would be the best thing.

Mairtin I don't need advice from you, Mick Dowd, on
not drowning on sick. I know well.

Mick Like this, now.

Mairtin I know like that, and your floor is filthy.

Mick This is what I always remember on going to bed,
no matter how much of a sup I've had, this is what I
always remember (*Almost tearfully.*) in mind of me three poor
uncles, were young men.

Mairtin Get up anyways, now, because it wasn't sick was
the subject at all. You do always be changing the subject
on me. Wee was the subject.

Mick (*getting up*) Three uncles, I'm saying.

Mairtin I know, three uncles.

Mick And one of them in America.

Mairtin In America? I suppose people do drown on their
sick in America too. Oh of course.

Mick In Boston Massachusetts.

Mairtin In Boston Massachusetts?

Mick In Boston Massachusetts. He did drown on his sick.

Mairtin I suppose at least he'd travelled. (*Pause.*) Good-
oh.

The two almost simultaneously begin smashing up the bones again.

Mick   We should have music as we're doing this.

Mairtin (*blankly*)   Music, music . . .

Mick   Music to hammer dead fellas to. I have a Dana record somewhere . . .

Mairtin   Put Dana on so.

Mick *puts on 'All Kinds of Everything' by Dana.*

Mick   I didn't think young people liked Dana nowadays.

Mairtin   They may not but I do. I've liked Dana since I was a child. If I met Dana I'd give her a kiss.

Mick   She wouldn't be kissing you, ya get.

Mairtin   For why?

Mairtin *stops hammering, looking sad and serious.* **Mick** *stops and looks at him.*

Mick   Why wouldn't Dana be kissing you?

Mairtin   Aye.

Mick (*pause*)   Well maybe she would, now.

Mairtin   On the lips.

Mick (*shrugging*)   Maybe she would.

Mairtin   Although she's a born-again Christian now.

Mick   Honestly, Mairtin, I'd avoid her.

Mick *starts hammering again, and after a few seconds* **Mairtin** *joins him.*

Mairtin (*pause*)   Would you be hammering your missus's bones with equal fervour were she here, Mick?

Mick   I wouldn't be. I'd have some respect.

Mairtin   Maybe a favour it was they did you so, the

fellas went and stole her on you?

Mick   No favour was it to me, and if I had the feckers here, then you'd be seeing some fancy skull-battering. I'll tell you that. Battered to dust they would be!

Mairtin   Good enough for them, the morbid oul fecks. And not only stealing your missus then, if that weren't enough, but to go pinching the locket that lay round her neck too, a locket that wouldn't fetch you a pound in the Galway pawn, I'd bet.

Mick *has stopped hammering on the locket's first mention and stepped back a pace, staring at* **Mairtin** *whose hammering continues unabated, entirely unaware of his faux-pas.*

Mick   The rose locket, was it?

Mairtin   The rose locket, aye, with the picture of you. What use would the fecks have in taking that, other than just to taunt you?

Mick *sits down in the armchair, the mallet in his lap, still staring at* **Mairtin***, who continues ahead with the skulls.*

Mairtin   The miserable heathen gets, and that's all they are. It was probably the same ones stole me *Star Wars* men on me when I was four, when I left them out in the rain. It was Han and Luke and . . . was it Chewie? No, I didn't have Chewie. It was Han and Luke and some other one they had off me . . . Princess Leia! Aye, and them are the three best ones in *Star Wars*. You can't play *Star Wars* without them. Look at you sitting there! Be getting back to work you, ya slack feck ya, or I'll have a word with oul Welsh Welsh to be docking your wages on you. Welsh.

Mick   In a minute now, Mairtin. I've to sit down and be having a think a minute.

Mairtin (*stopping hammering*)   That's what all the clever kids at school do do is sit down and be having a think, when it's out in the yard playing football they should be, and getting some sun on their arms. You can't budge the freckle-faced fecks, not even with a dig. (*Pause.*) Ah good

luck to them, they're not harming anyone. Why should I
be ordering them about and giving them digs? They've
every right to be sitting. (*Pause.*) I do get in an awful happy
mood when it's out of me brains I am, Mick.

Mick   I can see.

Mairtin   I could kiss fools and feck dogs. (*Pause.*) Have we
done enough hammering for the meantime so?

Mick   We have.

Mairtin   What's next on the agenda?

Mick   Be picking up a few of the big lumps, there, and
be putting them in the sack.

Mairtin *does so, drunkenly.*

Mairtin   Ah there's too many of the bastards to be
picking up. You should get a hoover.

Mick   Just a few more of the big ones will do us.

Mairtin   I was promised a dustpan and brush a while
back. I see that promise proved untrue. Now what?

Mick (*standing*)   Now we'll be driving them out to the lake
to be starting the disposing.

Mairtin   With a string of prayers said over them, Mick?

Mick   With a string of prayers said over them. I'll be
getting me car out now, unless I don't suppose you'd want
to be driving, Mairtin?

Mairtin   Ah you wouldn't let me be driving, would ya?

Mick   If you're not up to the job, no I wouldn't be.

Mairtin   I'd be up to the job, Mick! I'd be up to the job!

Mick   You're not a tadeen over the limit, now?

Mairtin   I'm not near the limit, sure. I've had a bare sip.
Oh let me be driving, Mick. Please now.

Pause. **Mick** *takes his car keys out of his pocket and tosses them to*

Mairtin, *who fumbles them at length and drops them, then drunkenly picks them back up off the floor.*

Mairtin   Oh jeebies, this has turned into a great oul night. Driving and drinking and skull-battering . . .

Mairtin *dashes out through the front door, leaving his sack behind him.*

Mick   Be bringing your bag of skulleens now, Mairtin!

Pause. **Mairtin** *returns slowly, smiling, and picks up the sack.*

Mairtin   I'd forget me head if it wasn't screwed up. *On.* Me mam does say 'You'd forget your head you would, Mairtin.' I say oh aye.

He exits with sack.

(*Off.*) I'll be sure and remember to be putting me seat-belt on too, Mick, knowing your track record.

Sound of **Mairtin** *laughing, off.*

Mick (*quietly*)   Be doing what you like, ya feck . . .

He picks up his mallet and rolls it around in his hand a little.

It'll make no difference in the end.

He exits briskly, bringing the mallet with him and turning the lights off behind him, as the sound of a car starting up is heard.

Scene Four

Mick *enters, turns lights on. His shirt is covered in blood. He wipes some blood off his mallet and lays it on the table, then brushes the bone fragments littering the floor into the next room. He sits in his armchair when finished. There is a knock at the door.* **Mick** *lets* **Maryjohnny** *in.*

Mary   Mick.

Mick   Maryjohnny.

Mary   Cold.

Mick I suppose it's cold.

Mary Oh, now, it's cold, Mick.

Mick Well, it's *night* I suppose.

Mary Oh it's night, aye.

Mick I suppose a sup would you be after?

Mary Ah only if you're having one, Mick, now.

Mick *pours them two glasses.*

Mary I've just come from the bingo.

Mick Oh aye, and how many times tonight did you win?

Mary Only three times tonight, Mick. One of me flourescent pens ran out on me.

Mick Uh-huh, that's always the worry with flourescent pens. You had a bad night of it so.

Mary Two free goes on the bumpy slides at the Leisureland swimming is all they gave me. I won't get much use out of them. (*Pause.*) You wouldn't want them, Mick?

Mick I wouldn't, Mary. I was never a man for bumpy slides. Never saw the sense in them.

Mary I'll give them to Mairtin or someone so. Is Mairtin able to swim?

Mick *wipes some of the blood from himself.*

Mick I'd bet money against it.

Mary What's all that on you, Mick? Out painting have you been?

Mick I have, aye. I've been out painting red things.

Mary That'll stain.

Mick Ah it's just an oul work-shirt, Maryjohnny. What harm?

Mary No harm. (*Pause.*) I heard tell of your Oona going missing on you, Mick. That was a terrible thing. If you can't be let rest when it's seven years dead you are, when can you be let rest.

Mick You can never be let rest.

Mary I couldn't bear to think of anyone running off with my bones when I'm dead.

Mick No one'll run off with your bones, Maryjohnny. Sure, they'd need a small truck to begin with.

Mary A small truck for why?

Mick No why. Just a biteen big-boned sometimes you do seem.

Mary I'm not big-boned. I'm just a bit fat is all.

Mick A bit fat, oh aye, aye. A bit fat indeed.

Mary It's a peculiar mood tonight you're in, Mick.

Mick It is. It must be them paint fumes or something.

Mary (*pause*) Did you hear Ray Dooley's lost his tour guide job?

Mick I did. Sure, if you go pegging shite at Americans you're bound to lose your tour guide job.

Mary You are.

Mick And cracking Vietnam jokes then.

Mary Off to Boston for his brother's wedding next month he is.

Mick Next month, is it? That wasn't a very long engagement. Me and Oona five years we were engaged, and it was five years we well needed. To get to know each other's faults and the like, y'know, and to accept them then.

Mary What was Oona's biggest fault, Mick?

Mick Oona didn't have big faults really. She just had

little faults. Niggly things, y'know? She'd never wrap up
cheese properly. Y'know, when she was finished with it.
She'd just leave it lying about, letting the air get to it. The
same with bread. She'd never wrap up bread properly.
Y'know, like after she'd made a sandwich or the like. And
she was terrible at scrambled eggs, and I don't know why,
because scrambled eggs are easy to do. Oona's scrambled
eggs'd come out either grey or burned.

Mary You don't miss her so.

Mick I *do* miss her. I mean, that scrambled egg business
wasn't really a big thing. We'd just avoid having scrambled
eggs, y'know? (*Pause.*) I miss the talk of her. Oona could fill
the house with talk. And she'd always stand up for me
against people. Y'know, in a fight or something, or if
people were saying things agin me. She'd've been the first
to defend me if she heard the town was saying I murdered
her on purpose.

Mary It's a shame she's dead so. (*Pause.*) I wonder who it
was took her?

Mick Uh-huh?

Thomas *knocks and enters, carrying a small bag.*

Mary Evening, Thomas. Cold.

Thomas What are you doing up here?

Mary I was passing on me way from the bingo.

Thomas I thought I told Father Welsh to bar you from
the bingo.

Mary You did but Father Welsh reinstated me to the
bingo.

Thomas So he countermanded official police orders, did
he? I'll have to be looking into that one. You run along
home now, Gran. I want to speak to Mick alone.

Mary I've only just got here, sure.

Thomas I don't care if you've only just got here. That's an official police order, I'm saying.

Mary   Don't you go official police ordering me, Thomas Hanlon, the number of times I wiped the dribbling skitter off the bare babby's backside of ya.

Thomas   *Please*, Gran.

Mary   I'll go when I've finished me sup and not before.

Mick   What would you want to be speaking to me alone for anyways?

Thomas   Oh nothing terrible important really. Just I'd like you to write out and sign a little oul confession for me, that's all. Just a weeny little confession, like.

Mick   A confession to what?

Thomas *takes a skull with a large forehead-crack out of his bag.*

Thomas   A confession to the murdering be blunt instrument, or be some sort of instrument, of your late wife, Mrs Oona Margaret Dowd.

Thomas *gestures to the skull crack.*

Mary   No . . . !

Mick   Oh. Okay so.

Thomas   Hah?

Mick   Okay, I said. Do ya have a pen?

Thomas   (*checks himself*)   I don't. Don't you have one?

Mick *looks for a pen.*

Mick   I have one somewhere, I know.

Mary   (*takes out bingo pens*)   I have me bingo pens. They're flourescent but they don't all work.

Thomas   Sure flourescent pens are no good for filling out confessions, sure!

Mary   A yalla one?

Thomas   No. 'A yalla one', Jesus.

Mick (*finding pen*)   Here, me lucky lotto pen. Now, what exactly do you want me to be saying, Thomas?

Thomas   Well, the *truth*, Mick.

Mick   Oh, the truth, aye. Fair enough.

Mick *writes out his confession on two pieces of paper* **Thomas** *gives him, as* **Mary** *picks the skull up.*

Mary   It's true? (*Pause.*) I had always prayed only fool gossiping is all it ever was. If I had known that . . .

Mick   If you had known that you'd still've come up cadging booze off me all these years, ya cheapskate fecking lump.

Thomas   Don't you go calling my granny a cheapskate fecking lump, ya murdering oul ghoul, ya.

Mick   Murdering oul what ya?

Thomas   Ghoul, ghoul.

Mick   Oh, ghoul. I thought you said 'whore'.

Thomas   And don't go criticising me pronunciation either!

Mick (*to* **Mary**)   You just put my wife's skull down now you, you and your flourescent fecking pens. Look at as many flourescent pens she has, Thomas, when bingo's supposed to be a bit of fun and a bit of fun to raise a few bob for them poor oul fecks in Africa. Out the mouths of starving darkies Maryjohnny rips her bingo winnings, but I see you don't go getting her confessing.

Mary   Isn't it better to starve darkies than to murder missuses?

Mick   Not at all is it better, and put my Oona down now, you, I've told you once. I don't want the pooh-stench of your manky hands grubbing all over her.

Mary *puts skull down and continues drinking.* **Mick** *writes.*

Mick   Where was it you found her, Thomas?

Thomas   Down the bottom of our fields I found her.

Mick   The bottom of yere fields, oh aye. Down beside the bones of that dead cow Mairtin was telling us about the other day, I'll bet. The one he said wandered in and fell down dead, when doesn't the world and his wife know he dragged that cow screaming from Pato Dooley's place and hit it with a brick, and it's only as easy-going as Pato is he never pressed charges.

Thomas   That's only circumstantial evidence.

Mick   No, that's only *hearsay* evidence.

Thomas   Feck I'm always getting them two beggars mixed up. What harm? It isn't knowing the difference between hearsay and circumstantial evidence that makes you a great copper. No. Detective work it is, and going hunting down clues, and never letting a case drop no matter what the odds stacked against you, no matter how many years old.

Mary   Like *Petrocelli*.

Thomas   Like *Petrocelli* is right, Gran, and the first thing I do when they promote me is reopen the case of that lettuce and jam man I was telling you about, 'cos I can't sleep nights sometimes thinking of that poor fella's murder going four years unsolved, as cold and alone in his big fat grave he lies.

Mick   And the fella who drowned on wee is another.

Thomas   And the fella who drowned on wee is another. I may bring a urine expert in on that one.

Mick   What's another word for 'convulse'? I've used 'convulse' once and I don't want to be repeating meself.

Thomas   (*thinking*)   Convulse, convulse, convulse . . . Spasm.

Mick   Spasm, spasm, spasm . . . Good one. (*Writes.*)

Thomas   I have a great vocabulary me, I do, oh aye. (*Pause.*) Are you nearly done?

Mick   I'm nearly done, all right.

Mary   Poor Oona. Why did you kill her, Mick? Sure, bad scrambled eggs is no just cause to butcher your wife.

Mick   I know it's not, Mary, and do you want to hear something funny? I *didn't* butcher my wife. Just like for seven long years I've been saying I didn't butcher my wife. I never butchered anybody 'til tonight.

He gives his confession to **Thomas***, who reads through it at speed.*

A pure, drink-driving was all my Oona was, as all along I've said, but if it's a murderer ye've always wanted living in yere midst, ye can fecking have one.

Thomas   D'you think I'm going to believe this pile of fecking bull?! Down the disco with Ray Dooley tonight Mairtin is, and nowhere but the disco.

Mick   But, sure, if down the disco Mairtin was, how would I have ended up with his bastard brains dripping down the bloody front of me?

Mary   No ...!

Mick   D'you see how great a copper he is, Maryjohnny, with his skills and his solving and his lettuces in empty fridges, yet doesn't bat an eye at a blood-soaked man standing whap-bang in front of the feck-brained fool ...

Thomas   You killed him?

Mick   I did, aye. His body's hanging halfway out the windscreen of me Anglia a mile away there.

Thomas *dives for* **Mick***, knocking him off his chair and strangling him on the floor,* **Mick** *barely defending himself.*

Mary   Leave him, Thomas, leave him! Thomas!

Mairtin *enters behind her, somewhat concussed, a big bloody crack down the centre of his forehead, dripping onto his shirt. He watches the fight a while,* **Mary** *noticing him after a few seconds, confused.*

Mairtin   What are them two gobshites up to?

Thomas *stops strangling* **Mick**. *Both stand and stare at* **Mairtin**.

Mairtin What are ye's feckers looking at? Ye's *fellas* looking at, I mean?

Thomas *examines* **Mairtin**'s *wound.* **Mary** *sits, refilling drink.*

Mary How are you, Mairtin?

Mairtin I'm fine, Gran, although a biteen of a headache I do have, aye. What are you doing pawing at me, you?

Thomas *rubs* **Mairtin**'s *face gently.*

Thomas We have you now, Michael Dowd. We have you now.

Thomas *takes his handcuffs out and goes to* **Mick**.

Mairtin Have him for what?

Thomas . Have him for ramming a mallet through the poor brains of you.

Mairtin A mallet? What are you talking about, sure? A pure drink-driving is all this was.

Thomas Hah?

Mick Hah?

Mairtin A pure drink-driving is all this was. What would Mick want to go malleting my poor brains for? Mick likes me an awful lot, don't you, Mick?

Mick I do, Mairtin. Sure I think you're a great fella.

Mairtin See, Thomas? Mick thinks I'm a great fella.

Behind **Thomas**'s *back,* **Mick** *picks up the confession and sets it alight. It slowly burns as* **Thomas** *questions* **Mairtin**.

Thomas Listen, Mairtin, concussed is all you are now, and who wouldn't be . . .

Mairtin I'm not at all concussed. It'd take more than a major car-crash to concuss me, I'll tell ya.

Thomas But didn't he just sign a confession saying he

hacked through the drunken skull of ya?

Mairtin   Did ya, Mick?

Mick   No, no, I didn't, Mairtin.

Mairtin   There you go.

Thomas   What d'you mean you didn't? Don't I have the fecking thing right here . . . ?

Thomas *turns to see the last corner of the confession burning to ash.*

Mick   You've cocked it up again, haven't ya?

Thomas   Mairtin? Listen to me. You're going to come down to the station with me, now, and you're going to swear out how Mick it was tried to kill you tonight . . .

Mairtin   Oh Jesus, can't you just leave poor Mick alone and in peace, you, *McMillan and Wife*?

Thomas   Don't keep calling me *McMillan and Wife*, I've told you twenty fecking times!

Mairtin   If he said he didn't kill his missus that's good enough for me, and let it rest.

Thomas   What are you on his fecking side for?!

Mairtin   Well why wouldn't I be on his fecking side, when it's me own blackguard brother I catch carving a hole in Mick's missus's skull there, the day after you'd dug her up on him.

Thomas   Shut up about that digging . . . !

Mairtin   I won't shut up about that digging and I'll tell you why I won't shut up about that digging! Because not even a fecking pound would the Galway pawn give me for that rose locket, and you said it'd get me at least ten.

He gives **Mick** *the locket.*

Only gave me that to shut me up, he did, Mick, but I realise that'd be nothing more than stealing from ya, and

not only stealing from ya but stealing from the poor dead
wife of ya, and anyways the fella in the pawn said it was
just a piece of shite not worth pissing on, so it's no great
loss, ya know what I mean, like?

Thomas Are you finished, Mairtin?

Mairtin (*pause. Confused*) Am I Finnish?

Thomas Are you *finished*, I said.

Mairtin Oh, am I finished? (*Thinks awhile.*) No I'm not
finished, Mr high-and-mighty detective bollocks. Heh,
detective me arse, when the whole of Leenane knows you'd
have trouble arresting a shop-lifting child, if the child
confessed with the chocolate round his gob. Or if you did
arrest him you'd arrest him for killing the Kennedys.

Thomas Is that right?

Mairtin It is. Sure it's only 'cos you're so good at
helping kids across the road that you're even tolerated in
this job.

Thomas You're finished now, are ya?

Mairtin I'm finished for the minute, aye, but I may be
thinking up some more insults for ya in a whileen once I
get me breath back.

Thomas But for the time being you're finished?

Mairtin For the time being I'm finished, aye. Sure
haven't I just said five times?

Thomas Good-oh.

Thomas *smashes* **Mairtin** *twice across the head with the mallet,*
Mairtin *collapsing to the floor.*

Mary Thomas!

Mick *forcibly restrains* **Thomas** *from hitting* **Mairtin** *any more.*

Mick Leave him, Thomas, Christ! Thomas!

Mairtin (*dazed*) What did he do that fer?

Thomas *stares at* **Mick** *blankly a while, sucking a second on his inhaler,* **Mick** *still holding him by the arms.*

Thomas I think . . . I think . . . I think they're never going to promote me.

Mick *lets* **Thomas** *go.* **Mairtin** *has crawled onto a chair. In a blank daze,* **Thomas** *caresses* **Mairtin**'s *cheek, then gently touches his bloody head.*

Mairtin (*quietly, worried*) Are you all right there, Tom?

Thomas *nods blankly.*

Thomas I'll get you for all this someday, Mick Dowd. On me own soul I swear it.

Mick Good luck so.

Thomas *nods, glances at the skull and at* **Mick**, *then exits.* **Mick** *sits with his wife's skull in his hands.* **Mary** *dabs at* **Mairtin**'s *bloody head with a hanky,* **Mairtin** *yelping slightly in pain.*

Mairtin Ar Gran, ya bitch!

Mary *tuts.*

Mairtin Ar Gran ya eejit, I meant. There'd better be none of your mouldy oul snot on that hanky now, Gran.

Mary There's not, Mairtin. This is just me hanky for show.

Mairtin Your hanky for show? Uh-huh?

He gives **Mick** *a look as if* **Mary** *is mad.*

D'ya hear this one?

Mick I think maybe to hospital you should be going for yourself, now, Mairtin. A bang on the head can be awful serious if not looked at.

Mairtin Ar hospitals are for poofs, sure.

Mick   Hospitals aren't for poofs. They let anybody in.

Mairtin   For poofs and for lesbos who can't take a middling dig.

Mary *tuts*.

Mairtin ˙ Wha? 'Lesbos' isn't swearing.

Mary   Is it not?

Mairtin   No. It's short for lesbians, y'know.

Mary   Oh.

Mairtin   'Lesbos'. Y'know, like Mona McGhee in me school with the beard. (*Pause.*) Five times I've asked that bitch out and she still won't go.

Mick   There's nothing the matter with lesbians, Mairtin. They're doing no harm to anybody.

Mairtin   They're not, I suppose. And they're great at tennis. Em, you can leave me now, Gran. You're sort of getting on me nerves now, so you are.

Mary *stops attending to* **Mairtin** *and watches* **Mick** *with skull a while.*

Mairtin   I suppose that'd be your missus, would it, Mick?

Mick   It would.

Mairtin   Uh-huh. Has she changed much since last you saw her?

Mick (*pause*)   She has, Mairtin.

Mairtin   Oh aye, it's been seven years, I suppose.

Mary (*pause*)   Do you like bumpy slides, Mairtin?

Mairtin   Bumpy slides? Where the hell did bumpy bloody slides come from?

Mary   I won two goes on the bumpy slides at Leisureland if you'd want to go.

Mairtin   You won't catch me going on the bumpy slides

with you, missus. I'd look a pure fool.

Mary   No, you could bring somebody else, I'm saying.

She gives **Mairtin** *the tickets.*

Mairtin   Oh. Aye. Thank you, Gran. Maybe Mona'd want to go. Heh, this has been a great oul day, this has. Drinking and driving and bumpy slides, and that oul battering them skulls to skitter was the best part of the whole day.

Mary *stares at* **Mick** *sternly.*

Mairtin   Would you need any help in giving your Oona a batter, Mick, or will you be handling that one yourself, now.

Mick   I'll be handling this one meself, Mairtin.

Mairtin   Good-oh.

Mick   And I'll be sending you a bill for the damage to me Anglia before the week's out.

Mairtin   Ar that's not fair, Mick.

Mick   Well life's not fair, Mairtin.

Mairtin (*confused slightly*)   It *is* fair. I like it anyways.

He gets to his feet and is overcome with dizziness. He sways around the room on weak legs and only manages not to collapse by clinging onto a wall.

Em, I think I might pop into that hospital after all. A biteen dizzy I am. I'll be seeing ye.

Mick   Be seeing you, Mairtin.

Mairtin (*pause*)   Be seeing you, Gran, I said!

Mary   Be seeing you, Mairtin.

Mairtin   Jeez, *deaf.*

Mairtin *takes a deep breath then staggers across the room, swaying, just making it out through the door, which he pulls behind him.*

Mary So you do hammer the bones to skitter so.

Mick Tonight was the first time ever that hammering happened, Maryjohnny, and only because wasn't I pure upset as Oona going missing on me . . .

Mary And you expect me to believe you, the lies you never stop spouting?

Mick What lies?

Mary A fool could see Mairtin's injuries were no accident.

Mick And, sure, didn't I admit that one outright, and sign a confession to the fact? How was that a lie?

Mary And the lies o'er your poor Oona's dying then.

Mick Oh you're still not going on about that fecking one, are ya? I have never lied o'er Oona dying. Never once.

Mary Oh no? I must've been mistaken what I saw that night so, as along the two of ye drove.

Mick What did you see? There was nothing to see.

Mary Oh I suppose there was nothing to see, now.

Mick If you've something to say to me, go ahead and say it outright and stop beating around the bush like a petrified fecking lummox. If you had seen anything made you think I'd killed Oona deliberate, why so would you've still come visiting me every night for the past seven year?

Mary *finishes off her poteen with a flourish and puts the glass down.*

Mick Oh, just to cadge me fecking booze, was it? Well be off on the road for yourself if that's the only reason you come here, with your hour-long weather bulletins and your Eamonn fecking Andrews spouting then. I never laid a finger on Oona, not from the day we married to the day she died, and if it's that you think you can upset me saying you saw something that night when there was nothing to see, then you've got another fecking think coming, girlie.

Mary   I'm saying nothing. Nothing at all am I saying. All I'm saying is you'll be meeting up with Oona again someday, Mick Dowd, and not just the bare skull but the spirit of her, and when you meet may down to the stinking fires of Hell she drag the rotten murdering bones of you, and may downhill from there for you it go. Goodbye to you now.

Mary *moves to the door.*

Mick   Maryjohnny?

Mary *turns.*

Mick   You've forgotten your flourescent pens, there.

She picks the pens up.

Mary   Thank you.

Mary *goes to the door again.*

Mick   And Maryjohnny? (*Pause.*) I didn't touch her. I swear it.

Mary *stares at him a moment, then exits.* **Mick** *looks at the rose locket then picks up the skull and stares at it a while, feeling the forehead crack. He rubs the skull against his cheek.*

Mick (*quietly*)   I swear it.

He caresses the skull again, then kisses the cranium gently. Lights fade to black.

The Lonesome West

The Lonesome West, a Druid Theatre Company/Royal Court Theatre co-production, was first presented at the Town Hall Theatre, Galway, on 10th June 1997, and subsequently opened at the Royal Court Theatre Downstairs on 19th July 1997. The cast was as follows:

Girleen Kelleher	Dawn Bradfield
Father Welsh	David Ganly
Coleman Connor	Maeliosa Stafford
Valene Connor	Brian F. O'Byrne

Directed by Garry Hynes
Designed by Francis O'Connor
Lighting design by Ben Ormerod
Sound design by Bell Helicopter
Music by Paddy Cunneen

Characters

Girleen Kelleher, *seventeen, pretty.*
Father Welsh, *thirty-five.*
Coleman Connor
Valene Connor

Setting: Leenane, a small town in Connemara, County Galway.

Scene One

The kitchen/living-room of an old farmhouse in Leenane, Galway. Front door far right, table with two chairs down right, an old fireplace in the centre of the back wall, tattered armchairs to its right and left. Door to **Coleman**'s *room in the left back wall. Door to* **Valene**'s *room far left. A long row of dusty, plastic Catholic figurines, each marked with a black 'V', line a shelf on the back wall, above which hangs a double-barrelled shotgun and above that a large crucifix. A food cupboard on the wall left, a chest of drawers towards the right, upon which rests a framed photo of a black dog. As the play begins it is day.* **Coleman**, *dressed in black, having just attended a funeral, enters, undoing his tie. He takes a biscuit tin out of a cupboard, tears off the Sellotape that binds its lid and takes out from it a bottle of poteen, also marked with a 'V'.* **Father Welsh**, *a thirty-five-year-old priest, enters just behind him.*

Welsh   I'll leave the door for Valene.

Coleman   Be doing what you like.

He pours two glasses as **Welsh** *sits at the table.*

You'll have a drink with me you will?

Welsh   I will, Coleman, so.

Coleman (*quietly*)   A dumb fecking question that was.

Welsh   Eh?

Coleman   I said a dumb fecking question that was.

Welsh   Why, now?

Coleman *gives* **Welsh** *his drink without answering and sits at the table also.*

Welsh   Don't be swearing today of all days anyway, Coleman.

Coleman   I'll be swearing if I want to be swearing.

Welsh   After us only burying your dad, I'm saying.

Coleman   Oh aye, right enough, sure you know best, oh aye.

Welsh (*pause*)   Not a bad turnout anyways.

Coleman   A pack of vultures only coming nosing.

Welsh   Come on now, Coleman. They came to pay their last respects.

Coleman   Did seven of them, so, not come up asking where the booze-up after was to be held, and Maryjohnny then 'Will ye be having vol-au-vents?' There'll be no vol-au-vents had in this house for the likes of them. Not while Valene holds the purse-strings anyways. If it was me held the purse-strings I'd say aye, come around for yourselves, even if ye are vultures, but I don't hold the purse-strings. Valene holds the purse-strings.

Welsh   Valene does be a biteen tight with his money.

Coleman   A biteen? He'd steal the shite out of a burning pig, and this is his poteen too, so if he comes in shouting the odds tell him you asked me outright for it. Say you sure enough demanded. That won't be hard to believe.

Welsh   Like an alcoholic you paint me as half the time.

Coleman   Well that isn't a big job of painting. A bent child with no paint could paint you as an alcoholic. There's no great effort needed in that.

Welsh   I never touched the stuff before I came to this parish. This parish would drive you to drink.

Coleman   I suppose it would, only some people don't need as much of a drive as others. Some need only a short walk.

Welsh   I'm no alcoholic, Coleman. I like a drink is all.

Coleman   Oh aye, and I believe you too. (*Pause.*) Vol-au-vents, feck. The white-haired oul ghoulish fecking whore. She's owed me the price of a pint since nineteen-seventy-fecking-seven. It's always tomorrow with that bitch. I don't care if she does have Alzheimer's. If I had a vol-au-vent I'd shove it up her arse.

Welsh   That's not a nice thing to be saying about a . . .

Coleman   I don't care if it is or it isn't.

Welsh (*pause*)   This house, isn't it going to be awful lonesome now with yere dad gone?

Coleman   No.

Welsh   Ah it'll be a biteen lonesome I'm sure.

Coleman   If you're saying it'll be a biteen lonesome maybe it *will* be a biteen lonesome. I'll believe it if you're forcing it down me throat and sure aren't you the world's authority on lonesome?

Welsh   Are there no lasses on the horizon for ye, now ye're free and easy? Oh I'll bet there's hundreds.

Coleman   Only your mammy.

Welsh   It's a beautiful mood today you're in. (*Pause.*) Were you never in love with a girl, so, Coleman?

Coleman   I was in love with a girl one time, aye, not that it's any of your fecking business. At tech this was. Alison O'Hoolihan. This gorgeous red hair on her. But she got a pencil stuck in the back of her gob one day. She was sucking it the pointy-end inwards. She must've gotten a nudge. That was the end of me and Alison O'Hoolihan.

Welsh   Did she die, Coleman?

Coleman   She didn't die, no. I wish she had, the bitch. No, she got engaged to the bastarding doctor who wrenched the pencil out for her. Anybody could've done that job. It didn't need a doctor. I have no luck.

Pause. **Welsh** *drinks some more.* **Valene** *enters with a carrier bag out of which he takes some new figurines and arranges them on the shelf.* **Coleman** *watches.*

Valene   Fibreglass.

Coleman (*pause*)   Feck fibreglass.

Valene   No, feck you instead of feck fibreglass.

Coleman   No, feck you two times instead of feck fibreglass . . .

Welsh   Hey now!! (*Pause*.) Jesus!

Valene   He started it.

Welsh (*pause*)   Tom Hanlon I see he's back. I was speaking to him at the funeral. Did Tom know yere dad?

Coleman   Slightly he knew dad. He arrested him five or six times for screaming at nuns.

Welsh   I remember hearing tell of that. That was an odd crime.

Coleman   Not that odd.

Welsh   Ah come on, now, it is.

Coleman   Oh if you say it is, Walsh, I suppose it is.

Valene   I do hate them fecking Hanlons.

Welsh   Why now, Val?

Valene   Why, is it? Didn't their Mairtin hack the ears off of poor Lassie, let him fecking bleed to death?

Coleman   You've no evidence at all it was Mairtin hacked the ears off of Lassie.

Valene   Didn't he go bragging about it to Blind Billy Pender?

Coleman   That's only hearsay evidence. You wouldn't get that evidence to stand up in a court of law. Not from a blind boy anyways.

Valene   I'd expect you to be agin me. Full well I'd expect it.

Coleman   That dog did nothing but bark anyways.

Valene   Well barking doesn't deserve ears chopped off, Coleman. That's what dogs are supposed to do is bark, if you didn't know.

Coleman   Not at that rate of barking. They're meant to ease up now and then. That dog was going for the world's fecking barking record.

Welsh   And there's plenty enough hate in the world as it is, Valene Connor, without you adding to it over a dead dog.

Valene   Nobody'll notice a biteen more hate, so, if there's plenty enough hate in the world.

Welsh   A nice attitude that is for a . . .

Valene   Feck off and sling your sermons at Maureen Folan and Mick Dowd, so, if it's nice attitudes you're after, Walsh. Wouldn't that be more in your fecking line?

Welsh *bows his head and pours himself another drink.*

Coleman   That shut the fecker up.

Valene   It did. You see how quick he is to . . . That's my fecking poteen now! What's the . . . eh?

Coleman   He did come in pegging orders for a drink, now. What was I supposed to say to him, him just sticking dad in the ground for us?

Valene   Your own you could've given him so.

Coleman   And wasn't I about to 'til I up and discovered me cupboard was bare.

Valene   Bare again, was it?

Coleman   Bare as a bald fella's arse.

Valene   Never unbare are your cupboards.

Coleman   I suppose they're not now, but isn't that life?

Welsh   And there's no such word as unbare.

Valene *stares at* **Welsh** *sternly.*

Coleman (*laughing*)   He's right!

Valene   Picking me up on me vocabulary is it, Welsh?

Coleman   It is, aye.

Welsh   I'm not now. I'm only codding ya, Val.

Valene   And shaking the hands of Mick and Maureen weren't you, too, I saw you at the grave there, and passing chit-chat among ye . . .

Welsh   I was passing no chit-chat . . .

Valene   A great parish it is you run, one of them murdered his missus, an axe through her head, the other her mammy, a poker took her brains out, and it's only chit-chatting it is you be with them? Oh aye.

Welsh   What can I do, sure, if the courts and the polis . . .

Valene   Courts and the polis me arse. I heard the fella you represent was of a higher authority than the courts and the fecking polis.

Welsh (*sadly*)   I heard the same thing, sure. I must've heard wrong. It seems like God has no jurisdiction in this town. No jurisdiction at all.

Valene *takes his bottle, mumbling, and pours himself a drink. Pause.*

Coleman   That's a great word, I think.

Valene   What word?

Coleman   Jurisdiction. I like J-words.

Valene   Jurisdiction's too Yankee-sounding for me. They never stop saying it on *Hill Street Blues*.

Coleman   It's better than unbare anyways.

Valene   Don't you be starting with me again, ya feck.

Coleman   I will do what I wish, Mr Figurine-man.

Valene   Leave me figurines out of it.

Coleman   How many more do ya fecking need?

Valene   Lots more! No, lots and lots more!

Coleman   Oh aye.

Valene   And where's me felt-tip pen, too, so I'll be giving them me 'V'?

Coleman   I don't know where your fecking felt-tip pen is.

Valene   Well you had it doing beards in me *Woman's Own* yesterday!

Coleman   Aye, and you wrenched it from me near tore me hand off.

Valene   Is all you deserved . . .

Coleman   You probably went hiding it then.

On these words, **Valene** *instantly remembers where his pen is and exits to his room. Pause.*

He's forever hiding things that fella.

Welsh   I'm a terrible priest, so I am. I can never be defending God when people go saying things agin him, and, sure, isn't that the main qualification for being a priest?

Coleman   Ah there be a lot worse priests than you, Father, I'm sure. The only thing with you is you're a bit too weedy and you're a terror for the drink and you have doubts about Catholicism. Apart from that you're a fine priest. Number one you don't go abusing five-year olds so, sure, doesn't that give you a head-start over half the priests in Ireland?

Welsh   That's no comfort at all, and them figures are overexaggerated anyways. I'm a terrible priest, and I run a terrible parish, and that's the end of the matter. Two murderers I have on me books, and I can't get either of the beggars to confess to it. About betting on the horses and impure thoughts is all them bastards ever confess.

Coleman   Em, only I don't think you should be telling me what people be confessing, Father. You can be excommunicated for that I think. I saw it in a film with Montgomery Clift.

Welsh   Do ya see? I'm shite sure.

Coleman   Too hard on yourself is all you are, and it's only pure gossip that Mick and Maureen murdered anybody, and nothing but gossip. Mick's missus was a pure drink-driving accident is unfortunate but could've happened to anybody . . .

Welsh   With the scythe hanging out of her forehead, now, Coleman?

Coleman   A pure drink-driving, and Maureen's mam only fell down a big hill and Maureen's mam was never steady on her feet.

Welsh   And was even less steady with the brains pouring out of her, a poker swipe.

Coleman   She had a bad hip and everybody knew, and if it's at anybody you should be pegging murder accusations, isn't it me? Shot me dad's head off him, point blank range.

Welsh   Aye, but an accident that was, and you had a witness . . .

Coleman   Is what I'm saying. And if Valene hadn't happened to be there to see me tripping and the gun falling, wouldn't the town be saying I put the barrel bang up agin him, blew the head off him on purpose? It's only because poor Mick and Maureen had no witnesses is why all them gobshites do go gossiping about them.

Valene *returns with his pen and starts drawing 'V's on the new figurines.*

Welsh   See? You do see the good in people, Coleman. That's what I'm supposed to do, but I don't. I'm always at the head of the queue to be pegging the first stone.

Valene   He's not having another fecking crisis of faith?

Coleman   He is.

Valene   He never stops, this fella.

Welsh   Aye, because I have nothing to offer me parish at all.

Coleman   Sure haven't you just coached the under-twelves football to the Connaught semifinals yere first year trying?

Welsh   Ah the under-twelves football isn't enough to restore your faith in the priesthood, Coleman, and we're a bunch of foulers anyway.

Coleman   Ye aren't. Ye're skilful.

Welsh Ten red cards in four games, Coleman. That's a world's record in girls' football. That'd be a record in boys' football. One of the lasses from St Angela's she's still in hospital after meeting us.

Coleman If she wasn't up for the job she shouldn't've been on the field of play.

Welsh Them poor lasses used to go off crying. Oh a great coach I am, oh aye.

Coleman Sissy whining bitches is all them little feckers are.

A rap on the front door, then **Girleen**, *a pretty girl of seventeen, puts her head round it.*

Girleen Are ye in need?

Valene Come in for yourself, Girleen. I'll be taking a couple of bottles off ya, aye. I'll get me money.

Valene *exits to his room as* **Girleen** *enters, taking two bottles of poteen out of her bag.*

Girleen Coleman. Father Welsh Walsh Welsh . . .

Welsh Welsh.

Girleen Welsh. I know. Don't be picking me up. How is all?

Coleman We've just stuck our dad in the ground.

Girleen Grand, grand. I met the postman on the road with a letter for Valene.

She lays an official-looking envelope on table.

That postman fancies me, d'you know? I think he'd like to be getting into me knickers, in fact I'm sure of it.

Coleman Him and the rest of Galway, Girleen.

Welsh *puts his head in his hands at this talk.*

Girleen Galway minimum. The EC more like. Well, a fella won't be getting into my knickers on a postman's wages. I'll tell you that, now.

Coleman   Are you charging for entry so, Girleen?

Girleen   I'm tinkering with the idea, Coleman. Why, are you interested? It'll take more than a pint and a bag of Taytos, mind.

Coleman   I have a three-pound postal order somewhere I never used.

Girleen   That's nearer the mark, now. (*To* **Welsh**.) What kind of wages do priests be on, Father?

Welsh   Will you stop now?! Will you stop?! Isn't it enough for a girl going round flogging poteen, not to go talking of whoring herself on top of it?!

Girleen   Ah, we're only codding you, Father.

She fluffs her fingers through **Welsh***'s hair. He brushes her off.*

(*To* **Coleman**.) He's not having another crisis of faith is he? That's twelve this week. We should report him to Jesus.

Welsh *moans into his hands.* **Girleen** *giggles slightly.* **Valene** *enters and pays* **Girleen**.

Valene   Two bottles, Girleen.

Girleen   Two bottles it is. You've a letter there.

Coleman   Buy me a bottle, Valene. I'll owe ya.

Valene (*opening letter*)   Buy you a bottle me arse.

Coleman   Do ya see this fella?

Girleen   You've diddled me out of a pound, Valene.

Valene *pays up as if expecting it.*

Valene   It was worth a go.

Girleen   You're the king of stink-scum fecking filth-bastards you, ya bitch-feck, Valene.

Welsh   Don't be swearing like that now, Girleen . . .

Girleen   Ah me hairy arse, Father.

Valene (*re letter*)   Yes! It's here! It's here! Me cheque! And look how much too!

Valene *holds the cheque up in front of* **Coleman**'s *face*.

Coleman   I see how much.

Valene   Do ya see?

Coleman   I see now, and out of me face take it.

Valene (*holding it closer*)   Do ya see how much, now?

Coleman   I see now.

Valene   And all to me. Is it a closer look you do need?

Coleman   Out of me face take that thing now.

Valene   But maybe it's closer you need to be looking now . . .

Valene *rubs the cheque in* **Coleman**'s *face*. **Coleman** *jumps up and grabs* **Valene** *by the neck.* **Valene** *grabs him in the same way.* **Girleen** *laughs as they struggle together.* **Welsh** *darts drunkenly across and breaks the two apart.*

Welsh   Be stopping, now! What's the matter with ye?

Welsh *gets accidentally kicked as the brothers part. He winces.*

Coleman   I'm sorry, Father. I was aiming at that feck.

Welsh   Hurt that did! Bang on me fecking shin.

Girleen   You'll know now how the lasses at St Angela's be feeling.

Welsh   What's the matter with ye at all, sure?

Valene   He started it.

Welsh   Two brothers laying into each other the same day their father was buried! I've never heard the like.

Girleen   It's all because you're such a terrible priest to them, Father.

Welsh *glares at her. She looks away, smiling.*

Girleen   I'm only codding you, Father.

Welsh   What kind of a town is this at all? Brothers fighting and lasses peddling booze and two fecking murderers on the loose?

Girleen   And me pregnant on top of it. (*Pause.*) I'm not really.

Welsh *looks at her and them sadly, moving somewhat drunkenly to the door.*

Welsh   Don't be fighting any more, now, ye's two. (*Exits.*)

Girleen   Father Walsh Welsh has no sense of humour. I'll walk him the road home for himself, and see he doesn't get hit be a cow like the last time.

Coleman   See you so, Girleen.

Valene   See you so, Girleen. (**Girleen** *exits. Pause.*) That fella, eh?

Coleman (*in agreement*)   Eh? That fella.

Valene   Jeez. Eh? If he found out you blew the head off dad on purpose, he'd probably get three times as maudlin.

Coleman   He takes things too much to heart does that fella.

Valene   Way too much to heart.

Blackout.

Scene Two

Evening. Against the back wall and blocking out the fireplace is now situated a large, new, orange stove with a big 'V' scrawled on its front. **Coleman**, *in glasses, sits in the armchair left, reading* Woman's Own, *a glass of poteen beside him.* **Valene** *enters, carrying a bag. Slowly, deliberately, he places a hand on the stove in a number of places in case it's been used recently.* **Coleman** *snorts in disgust at him.*

Valene   I'm checking.

Coleman   I can see you're checking.

Valene   I like to have a little check with you around.

Coleman   That's what you do best is check.

Valene   Just a biteen of a check, like. D'you know what I mean? In *my* opinion, like.

Coleman   I wouldn't touch your stove if you shoved a kettle up me arse.

Valene   Is right, my stove.

Coleman   If you fecking paid me I wouldn't touch your stove.

Valene   Well I won't be fecking paying you to touch me stove.

Coleman   I know well you won't, you tight-fisted feck.

Valene   And *my* stove is right. Did *you* pay the three hundred? Did *you* get the gas fixed up? No. Who did? Me. My money. Was it your money? No, it was my money.

Coleman   I know well it was your money.

Valene   If you'd made a contribution I'd've said go ahead and use me stove, but you didn't, so I won't.

Coleman   We don't even need a stove.

Valene   You may not need a stove, but I need a stove.

Coleman   You never fecking eat, sure!

Valene   I'll start! Aye, by Christ I'll start. (*Pause.*) This stove is mine, them figurines are mine, this gun, them chairs, that table's mine. What else? This floor, them cupboards, everything in this fecking house is mine, and you don't go touching, boy. Not without me express permission.

Coleman   It'll be hard not to touch your fecking floor, now.

Valene   Not without me express . . .

Coleman   Unless I go fecking levitating.

Valene   Not without me express . . .

Coleman   Like them darkies.

Valene (*angrily*)   Not without me express fecking permission I'm saying!

Coleman   Your express permission, oh aye.

Valene   To *me* all this was left. To me and me alone.

Coleman   Twasn't left but twas *awarded*.

Valene   Me and me alone.

Coleman   Awarded it was.

Valene   And you don't go touching. (*Pause.*) What darkies?

Coleman   Eh?

Valene   What darkies go levitating?

Coleman   Them darkies. On them carpets. Them levitating darkies.

Valene   Them's Pakies. Not darkies at all!

Coleman   The same differ!

Valene   Not at all the same differ! Them's Paki-men, same as whistle at the snakes.

Coleman   It seems like you're the expert on Paki-men!

Valene   I *am* the expert on Paki-men!

Coleman   You probably go falling in love with Paki-men too, so! Oh I'm sure.

Valene   Leave falling in love out of it.

Coleman   What did you get shopping, Mister 'I-want-to-marry-a-Paki-man'?

Valene   What did I get shopping, is it?

Valene *takes two figurines out of his bag and arranges them delicately on the shelf.*

Coleman   Ah for feck's sake . . .

Valene Don't be cursing now, Coleman. Not in front of the saints. Against God that is.

He takes eight packets of Taytos out of the bag and lays them on the table.

And some Taytos I got.

Coleman Be getting McCoys if you're getting crisps.

Valene I'll be getting what I li . . .

Coleman Ya fecking cheapskate.

Valene (*pause. Glaring*)   I'm not getting some crisps taste exactly the same, cost double, Coleman.

Coleman They don't taste the same and they have grooves.

Valene They do taste the same and feck grooves.

Coleman Taytos are dried fecking filth and everybody knows they are.

Valene The crisp expert now I'm listening to. What matter if they're dried fecking filth? They're seventeen pee, and whose crisps are they anyways? They're my crisps.

Coleman They're your crisps.

Valene My crisps and my crisps alone.

Coleman Or get Ripples.

Valene Ripples me arse and I don't see you digging in your . . . what's this?

Valene *picks up* **Coleman**'s *glass and sniffs it.*

Coleman What's wha?

Valene This.

Coleman Me own.

Valene Your own your arse. You've no money to be getting your own.

Coleman I do have.

Valene From where?

Coleman Am I being interrogated now?

Valene You are.

Coleman Feck ya so.

Valene *takes his poteen out of his biscuit tin to check if any is missing.* **Coleman** *puts the magazine aside, takes his glasses off and sits at the table.*

Valene You've been at this.

Coleman I haven't at all been at that.

Valene It seems very . . . reduced.

Coleman Reduced me arse. I wouldn't be at yours if you shoved a fecking . . .

Valene (*sipping it, uncertain*) You've topped it up with water.

Coleman Be believing what you wish. I never touched your poteen.

Valene Where would you get money for . . . Me house insurance?! Oh you fecker . . . !

Valene *desperately finds and examines his insurance book.*

Coleman I paid in your house insurance.

Valene This isn't Duffy's signature.

Coleman It is Duffy's signature. Doesn't it say 'Duffy'?

Valene You paid it?

Coleman Aye.

Valene Why?

Coleman Oh to do you a favour, after all the favours you've done me over the years. Oh aye.

Valene It's easy enough to check.

Coleman It *is* easy enough to check, and check ahead, ya feck. Check until you're blue in the face.

Confused, **Valene** *puts the book away.*

It's not only money can buy you booze. No. Sex appeal it is too.

Valene   Sex appeal? You? Your sex appeal wouldn't buy the phlegm off a dead frog.

Coleman   You have your own opinion and you're well entitled to it. Girleen's of the opposite opinion.

Valene   Girleen? Me arse.

Coleman   Is true.

Valene   Eh?

Coleman   I said let me have a bottle on tick and I'll be giving you a big kiss, now. She said 'If you let me be touching you below, sure you can have a bottle for nothing.' The deal was struck then and there.

Valene   Girleen wouldn't touch you below if you bought her a pony, let alone giving poteen away on top of it.

Coleman   I can only be telling the God's honest truth, and how else would I be getting poteen for free?

Valene (*unsure*)   Me arse. (*Pause.*) Eh? (*Pause.*) Girleen's pretty. (*Pause.*) Girleen's awful pretty. (*Pause.*) Why would Girleen be touching you below?

Coleman   Mature men it is Girleen likes.

Valene   I don't believe you at all.

Coleman   Don't so.

Valene (*pause*)   What did it feel like?

Coleman   What did what feel like?

Valene   The touching below.

Coleman   Em, nice enough now.

Valene (*unsure*)   I don't believe you at all. (*Pause.*) No, I don't believe you at all.

Coleman *opens and starts eating a packet of* **Valene**'s *crisps.*

Valene   Girleen wouldn't be touching you below. Never in the world would Girleen be touching y . . . (*Stunned.*) Who said you could go eating me crisps?!

Coleman   Nobody said.

Valene   In front of me?!

Coleman   I decided of me own accord.

Valene   You'll be paying me seventeen pee of your own accord so! And right now you'll be paying me!

Coleman   Right now, is it?

Valene   It is!

Coleman   The money you have stashed?

Valene   And if you don't pay up it's a batter I'll be giving you.

Coleman   A batter from you? I'd be as scared of a batter from a lemon.

Valene   Seventeen pee I'm saying!

Pause. **Coleman** *slowly takes a coin out of his pocket and, without looking at it, slams it down on the table.* **Valene** *looks at the coin.*

That's ten.

Coleman *looks at the coin, takes out another one and slams that down also.*

Coleman   You can keep the change.

Valene   I can keep the change, can I?

He pockets the coins, takes out three pee, opens one of **Coleman**'s *hands and places the money in it.*

I'm in no need of charity.

He turns away. Still sitting, **Coleman** *throws the coins hard at the back of* **Valene**'s *head.*

Ya fecker ya!! Come on so!

Coleman *jumps up, knocking his chair over.*

Coleman   Come on so, is it?

Valene   Pegging good money at me?!

Coleman   It is. And be picking that money up now, for your oul piggy-bank, ya little virgin fecking gayboy ya . . .

The two grapple, fall to the floor and roll around scuffling. **Welsh** *enters through the front door, slightly drunk.*

Welsh   Hey ye's two! Ye's two! (*Pause. Loudly.*) Ye's two!

Coleman (*irritated*)   Wha?

Welsh   Tom Hanlon's just killed himself.

Valene   Eh?

Welsh   Tom Hanlon's just killed himself.

Valene (*pause*)   Let go o' me neck, you.

Coleman   Let go o' me arm so.

The two slowly let go of each other and stand up, as **Welsh** *sits at the table, stunned.*

Welsh   He walked out into the lake from the oul jetty there. Aye, and kept walking. His body's on the shingle. His father had to haul me drunk out of Rory's to say a prayer o'er him, and me staggering.

Valene   Tom Hanlon? Jeez. Sure I was only talking to Tom a day ago there. The funeral.

Welsh   A child seen him. Seen him sitting on the bench on the jetty, a pint with him, looking out across the lake to the mountains there. And when his pint was done he got up and started walking, the clothes still on him, and didn't stop walking. No. 'Til the poor head of him was under. And even then he didn't stop.

Coleman (*pause*)   Ah I never liked that Tom fecking Hanlon. He was always full of himself, same as all fecking coppers . . .

Welsh (*angrily*)   The poor man's not even cold yet, Coleman Connor. Do you have to be talking that way about him?

Coleman   I do, or if I'm not to be a hypocrite anyways I do.

Valene   It's hypocrites now. Do you see this fella, Father? Ate a bag of me crisps just now without a by your leave . . .

Coleman   I paid you for them crisps . . .

Valene   Then says he's not a hypocrite.

Coleman   I paid thruppence over the odds for them crisps, and how does eating crisps make you a hypocrite anyways?

Valene   It just does. And interfering with a schoolgirl on top of it is another crime, Father.

Coleman   I interfered with no schoolgirl. I was interfered with *be* a schoolgirl.

Valene   The same differ!

Welsh   What schoolgirl's this, now?

Coleman   Girleen this schoolgirl is. This afternoon there she came up and a fine oul time we had, oh aye.

Welsh   Girleen? Sure Girleen's been helping me wash the strips for the under-twelves football all day, never left me sight.

Embarrassed, **Coleman** *gets up and moves towards his room.* **Valene** *blocks his way.*

Valene   Aha! Aha! Now who's the virgin fecking gayboy, eh? Now who's the virgin fecking gayboy?

Coleman   Out of me way, now.

Valene   *Now*, eh?

Coleman   Out of me way I'm saying.

Valene   I knew well!

Coleman   Are you moving or am I moving ya?

Valene   *Now* did I know well? Eh?

Coleman   Eh?

Valene   Eh?

Welsh   Coleman, come back now. We . . .

Coleman   And you can shut your fecking gob too, Welsh or Walsh or whatever your fecking name is, ya priest! You don't go catching Coleman Connor out on lies and expect to be . . . and be expecting to . . . to be . . .

Coleman *enters his room, slamming its door.*

Valene   You're a stuttering oul ass, so you are! 'To be . . . to be . . . to be . . .' (*To* **Welsh**.) Eh?

As **Valene** *turns back to* **Welsh**, **Coleman** *dashes out, kicks the stove and dashes back to his room,* **Valene** *trying and failing to catch him.*

Ya fecker, ya!

He checks the stove for damage.

Me good fecking stove! If there's any damage done to this stove it'll be you'll be paying for it, ya feck! Did you see that, Father? Isn't that man mad? (*Pause.*) Do ya like me new stove, Father? Isn't it a good one?

Coleman (*off*)   Do ya see that 'V' on his stove, Father? Do you think it's a V for Valene? It isn't. It's a V for Virgin, it is.

Valene   Oh is it now . . . ?

Coleman (*off*)   V for virgin it is, uh-huh.

Valene   When you're the king of the virgins?

Coleman (*off*)   Valene the Virgin that V stands for.

Valene   The fecking king of them you are! And don't be listening at doors!

Coleman (*off*)   I'll be doing what I wish.

Valene *checks stove again.* **Welsh** *is on the verge of tears.*

Valene (*re stove*)   No, I think it's okay, now . . .

Welsh   You see, I come in to ye . . . and ye're fighting. Fair enough, now, that's all ye two ever do is fight. Ye'll never be changed. It's enough times I've tried . . .

Valene   Are you crying, Father, or is it a bit of a cold you do have? Ah it's a cold . . .

Welsh   It's crying I am.

Valene   Well I've never seen the like.

Welsh   Cos I come in, and I tell ya a fella's just gone and killed himself, a fella ye went to school with . . . a fella ye grew up with . . . a fella never had a bad word to say about anybody and did his best to be serving the community every day of his life . . . and I tell you he's killed himself be drowning, is a horrible way to die, and not only do ye not bat an eye . . . not only do ye not bat an eye but ye go arguing about crisps and stoves then!

Valene   I batted an eye.

Welsh   I didn't notice that eye batted!

Valene   I batted a big eye.

Welsh   Well I didn't notice it, now!

Valene (*pause*)   But isn't it a nice stove, Father?

Welsh *puts his head in his hands.* **Valene** *goes to the stove.*

Valene   Only a day I've had it fixed up. You can still smell as clean as it is. Coleman's forbid to touch it at all because Coleman didn't contribute a penny towards it, for Coleman doesn't *have* a penny to contribute towards it. (*Picks up the three pee.*) He has three pee, but three pee won't go too far towards a stove. Not too far at all. He threw this three pee at me head earlier, d'you know? (*In realisation, angrily.*) And if he has no money and he wasn't interfered with, where the feck was it that poteen did come from?! Coleman . . . !

Welsh (*screamed*)   Valene, you fecking fecker ya!!

Valene   Wha? Oh, aye, poor Thomas.

Valene *nods in phoney empathy.*

Welsh (*pause. Sadly, standing*)   I came up to get ye to come to the lake with me, to be dragging poor Tom's body home for himself. Will ye be helping now?

Valene   I will be, Father. I will be.

Welsh (*pause*)   Feck. Two murders and a suicide now. Two murders and a fecking suicide . . .

Welsh *exits, shaking his head.*

Valene (*calling out*)   Sure, not your fault was it, Father. Don't you be getting maudlin again! (*Pause.*) Coleman? I'm off down . . .

Coleman (*off*)   I heard.

Valene   Are ya coming so?

Coleman (*off*)   Not at all am I coming. To go humping a dead policeman about the country? A dead policeman used to laugh at me press-ups in PE? I don't fecking think so, now.

Valene   You forever bear a grudge, you. Ah anyways it's good strong men Father Walsh does need helping him, not virgin fecking gayboys couldn't pay a drunk monkey to go interfering with him.

Valene *quickly exits.* **Coleman** *storms into the room to find him gone. He goes to the door and idles there, thinking, looking around the room. His gaze falls on the stove. He picks up some matches and opens the stove door.*

Coleman   A virgin fecking gayboy, is it? Shall we be having gas mark ten for no reason at all, now? We shall, d'you know?

He lights the stove, turns it up, closes its door and exits to his room. He returns a few seconds later and looks around the room.

For no reason at all, is it?

He takes a large oven-proof bowl out of a cupboard, places all of the figurines from the shelf into the bowl and puts the bowl inside the stove, closing its door afterwards.

Now we'll be seeing who's a virgin gayboy couldn't pay a
monkey to interfere with him. I'll say we'll fecking see.

*He pulls on his jacket, brushes his unkempt hair for two seconds with a
manky comb, and exits through the front door. Blackout.*

Scene Three

A few hours later. **Valene** *and* **Welsh** *enter, slightly drunk.*
Valene *takes his poteen out of his tin and pours himself a glass.*
Welsh *eyes it a little.*

Valene   That was an awful business, eh?

Welsh   Terrible. Just terrible, now. And I couldn't say a
thing to them. Not a thing.

Valene   What could be said to them, sure? The only thing
they wanted to hear was 'Your son isn't dead at all', and that
wouldn't have worked. Not with him lying in their front
room, dripping.

Welsh   Did you ever hear such crying, Valene?

Valene   You could've filled a lake with the tears that
family cried. Or a russaway at minimum.

Welsh (*pause*)   A wha?

Valene   A russaway. One of them russaways.

Welsh   Reservoir?

Valene   Russaway, aye, and their Mairtin crying with the
best of them. I've never seen Mairtin crying as hard. I
suppose that's all you deserve for chopping the ears off a poor
dog.

Welsh   I suppose if it's your only brother you lose you do
cry hard.

Valene   I wouldn't cry hard if I lost me only brother. I'd
buy a big cake and have a crowd round.

Welsh   Ah Valene, now. If it's your own brother you can't get on with, how can we ever hope for peace in the world . . . ?

Valene   Peace me arse and don't keep going on, you. You always do whine on this oul subject when you're drunk.

Valene *sits at the table with drink and bottle.*

Welsh (*pause*)   A lonesome oul lake that is for a fella to go killing himself in. It makes me sad just to think of it. To think of poor Tom sitting alone there, alone with his thoughts, the cold lake in front of him, and him weighing up what's best, a life full of the loneliness that took him there but a life full of good points too. Every life has good points, even if it's only . . . seeing rivers, or going travelling, or watching football on the telly . . .

Valene (*nodding*)   Football, aye . . .

Welsh   Or the hopes of being loved. And Thomas weighing all that up on the one hand, then weighing up a death in cold water on the other, and choosing the water. And first it strikes you as dumb, and a waste, 'You were thirty-eight years old, you had health and friends, there was plenty worse off fecks than you in the world, Tom Hanlon' . . .

Valene   The girl born with no lips in Norway.

Welsh   I didn't hear about her.

Valene   There was this girl in Norway, and she was born with no lips at all.

Welsh   Uh-huh. But then you say if the world's such a decent place worth staying in, where were his friends when he needed them in this decent world? When he needed them most, to say 'Come away from there, ya daft, we'd miss ya, you're worthwhile, as dumb as you are.' Where were his friends then? Where was I then? Sitting pissed on me own in a pub. (*Pause.*) Rotting in hell now, Tom Hanlon is. According to the Catholic Church anyways he is, the same as every suicide. No remorse. No mercy on him.

Valene   Is that right now? Every suicide you're saying?

Welsh   According to us mob it's right anyways.

Valene   Well I didn't know that. That's a turn-up for the books. (*Pause.*) So the fella from *Alias Smith and Jones*, he'd be in hell?

Welsh   I don't know the fella from *Alias Smith and Jones*.

Valene   Not the blond one, now, the other one.

Welsh   I don't know the fella.

Valene   He killed himself, and at the height of his fame.

Welsh   Well if he killed himself, aye, he'll be in hell too. (*Pause.*) It's great it is. You can kill a dozen fellas, you can kill two dozen fellas. So long as you're sorry after you can still get into heaven. But if it's yourself you go murdering, no. Straight to hell.

Valene   That sounds awful harsh. (*Pause.*) So Tom'll be in hell now, he will? Jeez. (*Pause.*) I wonder if he's met the fella from *Alias Smith and Jones* yet? Ah, that fella must be old be now. Tom probably wouldn't even recognise him. That's if he saw *Alias Smith and Jones* at all. I only saw it in England. It mightn't've been on telly here at all.

Welsh (*sighing*)   You wouldn't be sparing a drop of that poteen would ya, Valene? I've an awful thirst . . .

Valene   Ah, Father, I have only a drop left and I need that for meself . . .

Welsh   You've half the bottle, sure . . .

Valene   And if I had some I'd spare it, but I don't, and should priests be going drinking anyways? No they shouldn't, or anyways not on the night . . .

Welsh   Thou shouldst share and share alike the Bible says. Or somewhere it says . . .

Valene   Not on the night you let one of your poor flock go murdering himself you shouldn't, is what me sentence was going to be.

Welsh   Well was that a nice thing to be saying?! Do I need that, now?!

Valene (*mumbling*)   Don't go trying to go cadging a poor fella's drink off him so, the wages you're on.

Valene gets up, puts the bottle back in his biscuit tin and carefully sellotapes the lid up, humming as he does so.

Welsh   Is there a funny smell off of your house tonight, Val, now?

Valene   If you're going criticising the smell of me house you can be off now, so you can.

Welsh   Like of plastic, now?

Valene   Cadging me booze and then saying me house smells. That's the best yet, that is.

Welsh (*pause*)   At least Coleman came down to help us with poor Thomas after all, even if he was late. But that was awful wrong of him to go asking Tom's poor mam if she'd be doing vol-au-vents after.

Valene   That was awful near the mark.

Welsh   And her sitting there crying, and him nudging her then, and again and again 'Will ye be having vol-au-vents, Missus, will ye?'

Valene   If he was drunk you could excuse it, but he wasn't. It was just out of spite. (*Laughing.*) Although it was funny, now.

Welsh   Where is he anyways? I thought he was walking the road with us.

Valene   He'd stopped to do up his shoelaces a way back. (*Pause. In realisation.*) Coleman *has* no shoelaces. He has only loafers. (*Pause.*) Where have all me Virgin Marys gone?!

He leans in over the stove, placing his hands on its top, to see if the figurines have fallen down the back. The searing heat from the stove burns his hands and he pulls them away, yelping.

(*Hysterical.*) Wha?! Wha?!

Welsh   What is it, Valene? Did you go leaving your stove on?

Stunned, **Valene** *opens the stove door with a towel. Smoke billows out. He takes the steaming bowl of molten plastic out, sickened, places it on the table and delicately picks up one of the half-melted figurines with the towel.*

All your figurines are melted, Valene.

Valene (*staggering backwards*)   I'll kill the feck! I'll kill the feck!

Welsh   I'll be betting it was Coleman, Valene.

Valene   That's all there is to it! I'll kill the feck!

Valene *pulls the shotgun off the wall and marches around the room in a daze, as* **Welsh** *jumps up and tries to calm him.*

Welsh   Oh Valene now! Put that gun down!

Valene   I'll blow the head off him! The fecking head off him I'll blow! I tell him not to touch me stove and I tell him not to touch me figurines and what does he do? He cooks me figurines in me stove! (*Looking into bowl.*) That one was blessed be the Pope! That one was given me mammy be Yanks! And they're all gone! All of them! They're all just the fecking heads and bobbing around!

Welsh   You can't go shooting your brother o'er inanimate objects, Valene! Give me that gun, now.

Valene   Inanimate objects? Me figurines of the saints? And you call yoursel' a priest? No wonder you're the laughing stock of the Catholic Church in Ireland. And that takes some fecking doing, boy.

Welsh   Give it me now, I'm saying. Your own flesh and blood this is you're talking of murdering.

Valene   Me own flesh and blood is right, and why not? If he's allowed to murder his own flesh and blood and get away with it, why shouldn't I be?

Welsh   What are you talking about, now? Coleman shooting your dad was a pure accident and you know well.

Valene   A pure accident me arse! You're the only fecker in Leenane believes that shooting was an accident. Didn't dad make a jibe about Coleman's hairstyle, and didn't Coleman dash out, pull him back be the hair and blow the poor skulleen out his head, the same as he'd been promising to do since the age of eight and da trod on his Scalectrix, broke it in two . . .

Coleman *enters through the front door.*

Coleman   Well I did love that Scalectrix. It had glow in the dark headlamps.

Valene *turns and points the gun at* **Coleman**. **Welsh** *backs off moaning, hands to his head.* **Coleman** *nonchalantly idles to the table and sits down.*

Welsh   It can't be true! It can't be true!

Coleman   Look at that fella gone pure white . . .

Valene   No, shut up you! Don't be coming in mouthing after your fecking crimes . . .

Welsh   Tell me you didn't shoot your dad on purpose, Coleman. Please, now . . .

Valene   This isn't about our fecking dad! This is about me fecking figurines!

Coleman   Do you see this fella's priorities?

Valene   Melting figurines is against God outright!

Welsh   So is shooting your dad in the head, sure!

Valene   And on gas mark ten!

Welsh   Tell me, Coleman, tell me, please. Tell me you didn't shoot your dad there on purpose. Oh tell me, now . . .

Coleman   Will you calm down, you? (*Pause.*) Of course I shot me dad on purpose.

Welsh *starts groaning again.*

Coleman   I don't take criticising from nobody. 'Me hair's like a drunken child's.' I'd only just combed me hair and there was nothing wrong with it! And I know well shooting your dad in the head is against God, but there's some insults that can never be excused.

Valene   And cooking figurines is against God on top of it, if they're Virgin Mary figurines anyways.

Coleman   Is true enough, be the fella with the gun, and I'll tell you another thing that's against God, before this fella puts a bullet in me . . . (*To* **Welsh**.) Hey moany, are you listening . . . ?

Welsh   I'm listening, I'm listening, I'm listening . . .

Coleman   I'll tell you another thing that's against God. Sitting your brother in a chair, with his dad's brains dripping down him, and promising to tell everyone it was nothing but an accident . . .

Valene   Shut up now, ya feck . . .

Coleman   So long as there and then you sign over everything your dad went and left you in his will . . .

Welsh   No . . . no . . . no . . .

Coleman   His house and his land and his tables and his chairs and his bit of money to go frittering away on shitey-arsed ovens you only got to torment me, ya feck . . .

Welsh   No, now . . . no . . .

Valene   Be saying goodbye to the world, you, fecker!

Coleman   And fecking Taytos then, the worst crisps in the world . . .

Valene *cocks the gun that's up against* **Coleman**'s *head*.

Welsh   No, Valene, no!

Valene   I said say goodbye to the world, ya feck.

Coleman   Goodbye to the world, ya feck.

Valene *pulls the trigger. There is a hollow click. He pulls the trigger again. Another click. A third time, and another click, as* **Coleman** *reaches in his pocket and takes out two shotgun cartridges.*

Coleman   Do you think I'm fecking stupid, now? (*To* **Welsh**.) Did you see that, Father? My own brother going shooting me in the head.

Valene   Give me them fecking bullets, now.

Coleman   No.

Valene   Give me them bullets I'm saying.

Coleman   I won't.

Valene   Give me them fecking . . .

Valene *tries to wrench the bullets out of* **Coleman**'s *clenched fist,* **Coleman** *laughing as he does so.* **Valene** *grabs* **Coleman** *by the neck and they fall to the floor, grappling, rolling around the place.* **Welsh** *stares at the two of them dumbstruck, horrified. He catches sight of the bowl of steaming plastic beside him and, almost blankly, as the grappling continues, clenches his fists and slowly lowers them into the burning liquid, holding them under. Through clenched teeth and without breathing,* **Welsh** *manages to withhold his screaming for about ten or fifteen seconds until, still holding his fists under, he lets rip with a horrifying high-pitched wail lasting about ten seconds, during which* **Valene** *and* **Coleman** *stop fighting, stand, and try to help him . . .*

Valene   Father Walsh, now . . .

Coleman   Father Walsh, Father Walsh . . .

Welsh *pulls his fists out of the bowl, red raw, stifles his screams again, looks over the shocked* **Valene** *and* **Coleman** *in despair and torment, smashes the bowl off the table and dashes out through the front door, his fists clutched to his chest in pain.*

Welsh (*exiting, screaming*)   Me name's *Welsh*!!!

Valene *and* **Coleman** *stare after him a moment or two.*

Coleman   Sure that fella's pure mad.

Valene   He's outright mad.

Coleman   He's a lube. (*Gesturing at bowl.*) Will he be expecting us to clear his mess up?

Valene *puts his head out the front door and calls out.*

Valene   Will you be expecting us to clear your mess up, you?

Coleman (*pause*)   What did he say?

Valene   He was gone.

Coleman   A lube and nothing but a lube. (*Pause.*) Ah it's your fecking floor. You clean it up.

Valene   You wha?!

Coleman   Do you see me nice bullets, Valene?

Coleman *rattles his two bullets in* **Valene**'s *face, then exits to his room.*

Valene   Ya fecking . . . !

Coleman's *door slams shut.* **Valene** *grimaces, pauses, scratches his balls blankly and sniffs his fingers. Pause. Blackout.*

Interval.

Scene Four

A plain bench on a lakeside jetty at night, on which **Welsh** *sits with a pint, his hands lightly bandaged.* **Girleen** *comes over and sits down beside him.*

Welsh   Girleen.

Girleen   Father. What are ya up to?

Welsh   Just sitting here, now.

Girleen   Oh aye, aye. (*Pause.*) That was a nice sermon at Thomas's today, Father.

Welsh   I didn't see you there, did I?

Girleen   I was at the back a ways. (*Pause.*) Almost made me go crying, them words did.

Welsh You crying? I've never in all the years heard of you going crying, Girleen. Not at funerals, not at weddings. You didn't even cry when Holland knocked us out of the fecking World Cup.

Girleen Now and then on me now I go crying, over different things . . .

Welsh That Packie fecking Bonner. He couldn't save a shot from a fecking cow.

Welsh *sips his pint.*

Girleen I'd be saying you've had a few now, Father?

Welsh Don't you be starting on me now. On top of everybody else.

Girleen I wasn't starting on ya.

Welsh Not today of all days.

Girleen I wasn't starting at all on ya. I do tease you sometimes but that's all I do do.

Welsh Sometimes, is it? All the time, more like, the same as everybody round here.

Girleen I do only tease you now and again, and only to camouflage the mad passion I have deep within me for ya . . .

Welsh *gives her a dirty look. She smiles.*

Girleen No, I'm only joking now, Father.

Welsh Do ya see?!

Girleen Ah be taking a joke will ya, Father? It's only cos you're so high-horse and up yourself that you make such an easy target.

Welsh I'm not so high-horse and up meself.

Girleen All right you're not so.

Welsh (*pause*) *Am* I so high-horse and up meself?

Girleen No, now. Well, no more than most priests.

Welsh   Maybe I am high-horse so. Maybe that's why I don't fit into this town. Although I'd have to have killed half me fecking relatives to fit into this town. Jeez. I thought Leenane was a nice place when first I turned up here, but no. Turns out it's the murder capital of fecking Europe. Did *you* know Coleman had killed his dad on purpose?

Girleen (*lowers head, embarrassed*)   I think I did hear a rumour somewhere along the line . . .

Welsh   A fecking rumour? And you didn't bat an eye or go reporting it?

Girleen   Sure I'm no fecking stool-pigeon and Coleman's dad was always a grumpy oul feck. He did kick me cat Eamonn there once.

Welsh   A fella deserves to die, so, for kicking a cat?

Girleen (*shrugs*)   It depends on the fella. And the cat. But there'd be a lot less cats kicked in Ireland, I'll tell ya, if the fella could rest-assured he'd be shot in the head after.

Welsh   You have no morals at all, it seems, Girleen.

Girleen   I have plenty of morals only I don't keep whining on about them like some fellas.

Welsh (*pause*)   Val and Coleman'll kill each other someday if somebody doesn't do something to stop them. It won't be me who stops them anyways. It'll be someone with guts for the job.

He takes out a letter and passes it to **Girleen**.

I've written them a little lettereen here, Girleen, would you give it to them next time you see them?

Girleen   Won't you be seeing them soon enough yourself?

Welsh   I won't be. I'm leaving Leenane tonight.

Girleen   Leaving for where?

Welsh   Anywhere. Wherever they send me. Anywhere but here.

Girleen   But why, Father?

Welsh   Ah lots of different reasons, now, but the three slaughterings and one suicide amongst me congregation didn't help.

Girleen   But none of that was your fault, Father.

Welsh   Oh no?

Girleen   And don't you have the under-twelves semifinal tomorrow morning to be coaching?

Welsh   Them bitches have never listened to me advice before. I don't see why they should go starting now. Nobody ever listens to my advice. Nobody ever listens to me at all.

Girleen   I listen to you.

Welsh (*sarcastic*)   Ar that's great comfort.

Girleen bows her head, hurt.

Welsh   And you don't listen to me either. How many times have I told you to stop flogging your dad's booze about town, and still you don't?

Girleen   Ah it's just 'til I save up a few bob, Father, I'm doing that flogging.

Welsh   A few bob for what? To go skittering it away the clubs in Carraroe, and drunk schoolboys pawing at ya.

Girleen   Not at all, Father. I do save it to buy a few nice things out me mam's Freeman's catalogue. They do have an array of . . .

Welsh   To go buying shite, aye. Well I wish I did have as tough problems in my life as you do in yours, Girleen. It does sound like life's a constant torment for ya.

*Girleen stands up and wrenches **Welsh**'s head back by the hair.*

Girleen   If anybody else went talking to me that sarcastic I'd punch them in the fecking eye for them, only if I punched you in the fecking eye you'd probably go crying like a fecking girl!

Welsh   I never asked you to come sitting beside me.

Girleen   Well I didn't know there was a law against sitting beside ya, although I wish there fecking was one now.

Girleen *releases him and starts walking away.*

Welsh   I'm sorry for being sarcastic to you, Girleen, about your mam's catalogue and whatnot. I am.

Girleen *stops, pauses, and idles back to the bench.*

Girleen   It's okay.

Welsh   It's only that I'm feeling a bit . . . I don't know . . .

Girleen (*sitting beside him*)   Maudlin.

Welsh   Maudlin. Maudlin is right.

Girleen   Maudlin and lonesome. The maudlin and lonesome Father Walsh. *Welsh.* (*Pause.*) I'm sorry, Father.

Welsh   Nobody ever remembers.

Girleen   It's just Walsh is so close to Welsh, Father.

Welsh   I know it is. I know it is.

Girleen   What's your first name, Father?

Welsh (*pause*)   Roderick.

Girleen *stifles laughter.* **Welsh** *smiles.*

Girleen   Roderick? (*Pause.*) Roderick's a horrible name, Father.

Welsh   I know, and thanks for saying so, Girleen, but you're just trying to boost me spirits now, aren't ya?

Girleen   I'm just being nice to ya now.

Welsh   What kind of a name's Girleen for a girl anyways? What's your proper first name?

Girleen (*cringing*)   Mary.

Welsh (*laughing*)   Mary? And you go laughing at Roderick then?

Girleen   Mary's the name of the mammy of Our Lord, did you ever hear tell of it?

Welsh   I heard of it somewhere along the line.

Girleen   It's the reason she never got anywhere for herself. Fecking Mary.

Welsh   *You'll* be getting somewhere for yourself, Girleen.

Girleen   D'ya think so, now?

Welsh   As tough a get as you are? Going threatening to thump priests? Of course.

Girleen *brushes the hair out of* **Welsh***'s eyes.*

Girleen   I wouldn't have gone thumping you, now, Father.

She gently slaps his cheek.

Maybe a decent slapeen, now.

Welsh *smiles and faces front.* **Girleen** *looks at him, then away, embarrassed.*

Welsh (*pause*)   No, I just came out to have a think about Thomas before I go on me way. Say a little prayer for him.

Girleen   It's tonight you're going?

Welsh   It's tonight, aye. I said to meself I'll stay for Tom's funeral, then that'll be the end of it.

Girleen   But that's awful quick. No one'll have a chance to wish you goodbye, Father.

Welsh   Goodbye, aye, and good riddance to the back of me.

Girleen   Not at all.

Welsh   No?

Girleen   No.

Pause. **Welsh** *nods, unconvinced, and drinks again.*

Will you write to me from where you're going and be giving me your new address, Father?

Welsh   I'll try, Girleen, aye.

Girleen   Just so's we can say hello now and then, now.

Welsh   Aye, I'll try.

As he speaks, **Girleen** *manages to stifle tears without him noticing.*

This is where he walked in from, d'you know? Poor Tom. Look at as cold and bleak as it is. Do you think it took courage or stupidity for him to walk in, Girleen?

Girleen   Courage.

Welsh   The same as that.

Girleen   And Guinness.

Welsh (*laughing*)   The same as that. (*Pause.*) Look at as sad and as quiet and still.

Girleen   It's more than Thomas has killed himself here down the years, d'you know, Father? Three other fellas walked in here, me mam was telling me.

Welsh   Is that right now?

Girleen   Years and years ago this is. Maybe even famine times.

Welsh   Drowned themselves?

Girleen   This is where they all come.

Welsh   We should be scared of their ghosts so but we're not scared. Why's that?

Girleen   You're not scared because you're pissed to the gills. I'm not scared because . . . I don't know why. One, because you're here, and two, because . . . I don't know. I don't be scared of cemeteries at night either. The opposite of that, I do *like* cemeteries at night.

Welsh   Why, now? Because you're a morbid oul tough?

Girleen (*embarrassed throughout*)   Not at all. I'm not a tough. It's because . . . even if you're sad or something, or lonely or something, you're still better off than them lost in the ground or in the lake, because . . . at least you've got the *chance* of being happy, and even if it's a real little chance, it's more than them dead ones have. And it's not that you're saying 'Hah, I'm better than ye', no, because in the long run it might end up that you have a worse life than ever they had and you'd've been better off as dead as them, there and then. But at least when you're still here there's the *possibility* of happiness, and it's like them dead ones know that, and they're happy for you to have it. They say 'Good luck to ya.' (*Quietly.*) Is the way I see it anyways.

Welsh   You have a million thoughts going on at the back of them big brown eyes of yours.

Girleen   I never knew you did ever notice me big brown eyes. Aren't they gorgeous, now?

Welsh   You'll grow up to be a mighty fine woman one day, Girleen, God bless you.

Welsh *drinks again.*

Girleen (*quietly, sadly*)   One day, aye. (*Pause.*) I'll be carrying on the road home for meself now, Father. Will you be staying or will you be walking with me?

Welsh   I'll be staying a biteen longer for meself, Girleen. I'll be saying that prayer for poor Thomas, now.

Girleen   It's goodbye for a while so.

Welsh   It is.

Girleen *kisses his cheek and they hug.* **Girleen** *stands.*

Welsh   You'll remember to be giving that letter to Valene and Coleman, now, Girleen?

Girleen   I will. What's in it, Father? It does sound very mysterious. It wouldn't be packed full of condoms for them, would it?

Welsh   It wouldn't at all, now!

Girleen   Cos, you know, Valene and Coleman'd get no use out of them, unless they went using them on a hen.

Welsh   Girleen, now . . .

Girleen   And it'd need to be a blind hen.

Welsh You do have a terrible mouth on ya.

Girleen Aye, all the better to . . . no, I won't be finishing that sentence. Did you hear tell of Valene's new hobby, Father? He's been roaming the entirety of Connemara picking up new figurines of the saints for himself, but only ceramic and china ones won't go melting away on him. Thirty-seven of them at last count he has, and only to go tormenting poor Coleman.

Welsh Them two, they're just odd.

Girleen They *are* odd. They're the kings of odd. (*Pause.*) See you so, Father.

Welsh See you so, Girleen. Or Mary, is it?

Girleen If you let me know where you get to I'll write with how the under-twelves get on tomorrow. It may be in the *Tribune* anyways. Under 'Girl decapitated in football match'.

Welsh *nods, half smiles.* **Girleen** *idles away.*

Welsh Girleen, now? Thanks for coming sitting next to me. It's meant something to me, it has.

Girleen Any time, Father. Any time.

Girleen *exits.* **Welsh** *stares out front again.*

Welsh (*quietly*)   No, not any time, Girleen. Not any time.

Welsh *finishes his pint, puts the glass down, blesses himself and sits there quietly a moment, thinking. Blackout.*

Scene Five

Stage in darkness apart from **Welsh**, *who recites his letter rapidly.*

Welsh Dear Valene and Coleman, it is Father Welsh here. I am leaving Leenane for good tonight and I wanted to be saying a few words to you, but I won't be preaching at you for why would I be? It has never worked in the past and it won't work now. All I want to do is be pleading with you as a fella concerned about ye and ye're lives, both in this world

and the next, and the next won't be too long away for ye's if
ye keep going on as mad as ye fecking have been. Coleman, I
will not be speaking here about your murdering of your dad,
although obviously it does concern me, both as a priest and
as a person with even the vaguest moral sense, but that is a
matter for your own conscience, although I hope some day
you will realise what you have done and go seeking
forgiveness for it, because let me tell you this, getting your
hairstyle insulted is no just cause to go murdering someone,
in fact it's the worst cause I did ever hear. But I will leave it at
that although the same goes for you, Valene, for your part in
your dad's murdering, and don't go saying you had no part
because you did have a part and a big part. Going lying that
it was an accident just to get your father's money is just as
dark a deed as Coleman's deed, if not more dark, for
Coleman's deed was done out of temper and spite, whereas
your deed was done out of being nothing but a money-
grubbing fecking miser with no heart at all, but I said I
would not be preaching at you and I have lost me thread
anyways so I will stop preaching at you and be starting a new
paragraph. (*Pause*.) Like I said, I am leaving tonight, but I
have been thinking about ye non-stop since the night I did
scald me hands there at yeres. Every time the pain does go
through them hands I do think about ye, and let me tell you
this. I would take that pain and pain a thousand times worse,
and bear it with a smile, if only I could restore to ye the love
for each other as brothers ye do so woefully lack, that must
have been there some day. Didn't as gasurs ye love each
other? Or as young men, now? Where did it all go on ye?
Don't ye ever think about it? What I think I think what ye've
done is bury it deep down in ye, under a rack of grudges and
hate and sniping like a pair of fecking oul women. Ye two are
like a pair of fecking oul women, so ye are, arging over
fecking Taytos and stoves and figurines, is an arse-brained
argument. But I do think that yere love is still there under all
of that, in fact I'd go betting everything that's dear to me on
it, and may I rot in hell for ever if I'm wrong. All it is is ye've
lived in each other's pockets the entire of yere lives, and a
sad and lonesome existence it has been, with no women to

enter the picture for either of ye to calm ye down, or anyways not many women or the wrong sort of women, and what's happened the bitterness has gone building up and building up without check, the daily grudges and faults and moans and baby-crimes against each other ye can never seem to step back from and see the love there underneath and forgive each other for. Now, what the point of me letter is, couldn't ye do something about it? Couldn't the both of ye, now, go stepping back and be making a listeen of all the things about the other that do get on yere nerves, and the wrongs the other has done all down through the years that you still hold against him, and be reading them lists out, and be discussing them openly, and be taking a deep breath then and be forgiving each other them wrongs, no matter what they may be? Would that be so awful hard, now? It would for ye two, I know, but couldn't ye just be trying it, now? And if it doesn't work it doesn't work, but at least ye could say ye'd tried and would ye be any worse off? And if ye wouldn't be doing it for yourselves, wouldn't ye be doing it for me, now? For a friend of yeres, who cares about ye, who doesn't want to see ye blowing the brains out of each other, who never achieved anything as a priest in Leenane, in fact the opposite, and who'd see ye two becoming true brothers again as the greatest achievement of his whole time here. Sure it would be bordering on the miraculous. I might be canonised after. (*Pause.*) Valene and Coleman, I'm betting everything on ye. I know for sure there's love there somewheres, it's just a case of ye stepping back and looking for it. I'd be willing to bet me own soul that that love is there, and I know well the odds are stacked against me. They're probably 64,000 to one be this time, but I'd go betting on ye's still, for despite everything, despite yere murder and yere mayhem and yere miserliness that'd tear the teeth out of broken goats, I have faith in ye. You wouldn't be letting me down now, would ye? Yours sincerely, and yours with the love of Christ now, Roderick Welsh.

Pause. **Welsh** *shivers slightly. Blackout.*

Scene Six

Valene'*s house. Shotgun back on wall, over shelf full of new ceramic figurines, all marked with a 'V'.* **Coleman***, in glasses, sits in the armchair left, glass of poteen beside him, perusing another women's magazine.* **Valene** *enters carrying a bag and places his hand on the stove in a number of places. Irritated,* **Coleman** *tries to ignore him.*

Valene   I'm checking. (*Pause.*) It's good to have a little check. (*Pause.*) *I* think it is, d'you know? (*Pause.*) Just a *little* check. D'you know what I mean, like?

After a while more of this, **Valene** *takes some new ceramic figurines out of his bag, which he arranges with the others on the shelf.*

Coleman   Ah for . . .

Valene   Eh?

Coleman   Eh?

Valene   Now then, eh?

Coleman   Uh-huh?

Valene   Eh? Nice, I think. Eh? What do *you* think, Coleman?

Coleman   I think you can go feck yourself.

Valene   No, not feck meself at all, now. Or over to the left a biteen would they look better? Hmm, we'll put the new St Martin over here, so it balances out with the other St Martin over there, so's we have one darkie saint on either side, so it balances out symmetrical, like. (*Pause.*) I'm a great one for shelf arranging I am. It is a skill I did never know I had. (*Pause.*) Forty-six figurines now. I'm sure to be getting into heaven with this many figurines in me house.

Valene *finds his pen and marks up the new figurines.*

Coleman (*pause*)   There's a poor girl born in Norway here with no lips.

Valene (*pause*)   That's old news that lip girl is.

Coleman   That girl'll never be getting kissed. Not with the bare gums on her flapping.

Valene   She's the exact same as you, so, if she'll never be getting kissed, and you've no excuse. You've the full complement of lips.

Coleman   I suppose a million girls you've kissed in your time. Oh aye.

Valene   Nearer two million.

Coleman   Two million, aye. And all of them aunties when you was twelve.

Valene   Not aunties at all. Proper women.

Coleman   Me brother Valentine does be living in his own little dream-world, with the sparrows and the fairies and the hairy little men. Puw-ooh! And the daisy people.

Valene (*pause*)   I hope that's not my poteen.

Coleman   It's not at all your poteen.

Valene   Uh-huh? (*Pause.*) Did you hear the news?

Coleman   I did. Isn't it awful?

Valene   It's a disgrace. It's an outright disgrace, and nothing but. You can't go sending off an entire girl's football team, sure.

Coleman   Not in a semi-fecking-final anyways.

Valene   Not at any time, sure. If you have to send people off you send them off one at a time, for their individual offences. You don't go slinging the lot of them off wholesale, and only seven minutes in, so they go crying home to their mammys.

Coleman   St Josephine's have only got through be default, and nothing but default. If they had any honour they'd not take their place in the final at all and be giving it to us.

Valene   I hope they lose the final.

Coleman   The same as that, *I* hope they lose the final. Sure, with their goalie in a coma they're bound to.

Valene   No, their goalie came out of her coma a while ago there. Intensive care is all she's in now.

Coleman   She was fecking feigning? Getting us expelled from all competitions for no reason at all? I hope she relapses into her coma and dies.

Valene   The same as that, *I* hope she lapses into her coma and dies. (*Pause.*) Look at us, we're in agreement.

Coleman   We are, I suppose.

Valene   We can agree sometimes.

He snatches the magazine out of **Coleman**'s *hands.*

Except don't go reading me magazines, I've told you, 'til I've finished reading them.

He sits at the table and flips through the magazine without reading it. **Coleman** *fumes.*

Coleman (*standing*)   And don't go . . . don't go tearing them out of me fecking hands, near tore the fingers off me!

Valene   Have these fingers you (*V-sign.*) and take them to bed with ya.

Coleman   You're not even reading that *Take a Break*.

Valene   I *am* reading this *Take a Break*, or anyways I'm glancing through this *Take a Break* at me own pace, as a fella's free to do if it's with his own money he goes buying his *Take a Break*.

Coleman   Only women's magazines is all you ever go reading. Sure without doubt it's a fecking gayboy you must be.

Valene   There's a lad here in Bosnia and not only has he no arms but his mammy's just died. (*Mumbles as he reads, then:*) Ah they're only after fecking money, the same as ever.

Coleman   And no fear of you sending that poor no-armed boy any money, ah no.

Valene   They've probably only got him to put his arms behind his back, just to cod ya.

Coleman   It's any excuse for you.

Valene   And I bet his mammy's fine.

Coleman (*pause*)   Get *Bella* if you're getting magazines. *Take a Break*'s nothing but quizzes.

Valene   There's a coupon here for Honey Nut Loops.

Valene *starts carefully tearing out the coupon at the same time as* **Coleman** *quietly takes some Taytos out of a cupboard.*

Coleman   Quizzes and deformed orphans. (*Pause.*) Em, would you let me be having a bag of Taytos, Val? I'm hungry a biteen.

Valene (*looking up. Pause*)   Are you being serious, now?

Coleman   G'wan. I'll owe you for them.

Valene   Put that bag back, now.

Coleman   I'll owe you for them, I'm saying. You can put them on the same bill you've put your melted figurines.

Valene   Put them . . . put them . . . What are you doing, now? Put them Taytos back, I said.

Coleman   Valene, listen to me . . .

Valene   No . . .

Coleman   I'm hungry and I need some Taytos. Didn't I wait 'til you came back in to ask you, now, and only because I'm honest . . .

Valene   And you've asked me and I've said no. Slinging insults at me Taytos the other week I remember is all you were. I see the boot's on the other foot now.

Coleman   I've asked polite, now, Valene, and feck boots. Three times I've asked polite.

Valene   I know well you've asked polite, Coleman. You've asked awful polite. And what I'm saying to ya, ya can't have any of me fecking Taytos, now!

Coleman   Is that your final word on the subject?

Valene   It *is* me final word on the subject.

Coleman (*pause*)   I won't have any of your Taytos so. (*Pause.*) I'll just crush them to skitter.

He crushes the crisps to pulp and tosses the packet at **Valene**. **Valene** *darts up and around the table to get at* **Coleman**, *during which time* **Coleman** *grabs two more packets from the cupboard and holds them up, one in each hand, threatening to crush them also.*

Back off!

Valene *stops dead in his tracks.*

Coleman   Back off or they'll be getting it the same!

Valene (*scared*)   Be leaving me crisps now, Coleman.

Coleman   Be leaving them, is it? When all I wanted was to go buying one of them and would've paid the full whack, but oh no.

Valene (*tearfully, choking*)   That's a waste of good food that is, Coleman.

Coleman   Good food, is it?

Valene   There's Bosnians'd be happy to have them Taytos.

Coleman *opens one of the bags and starts eating just as the front door bangs open and* **Girleen** *enters, face blotchy, letter in hand.*

Coleman   They *are* good food, d'you know?

Girleen (*in shock throughout*)   Have ye heard the news, now?

Coleman   What news, Girleen? The under-twelves . . . ?

Seeing **Coleman** *distracted,* **Valene** *dives for his neck, trying to get the crisps off him at the same time. They drag each other to the floor, rolling and scuffling,* **Coleman** *purposely mashing up the crisps any chance he gets.* **Girleen** *stares at them a while, then quietly takes a butcher's knife out of one of the drawers, goes over to them, pulls* **Coleman**'s *head back by the hair and puts the knife to his neck.*

Valene   Leave Coleman alone, Girleen. What are you doing, now?

Girleen   I'm breaking ye up.

Coleman (*scared*)   We're broke up.

Valene (*scared*)   We're broke up.

Once the two are separated, **Girleen** *lets* **Coleman** *go and puts the letter on the table, sadly.*

Girleen   There's a letter there Father Welsh wrote ye.

Valene   What does that feck want writing to us?

Coleman   Going moaning again, I'll bet.

Valene *picks the letter up,* **Coleman** *pulls it off him,* **Valene** *pulls it back. They stand reading it together,* **Coleman** *getting bored after a few seconds.* **Girleen** *takes out a heart pendant on a chain and looks at it.*

Girleen   I read it already on ye, coming over. All about the two of ye loving each other as brothers it is.

Coleman (*stifling laughter*)   Wha?

Valene   Father Walsh Welsh's leaving, it looks like.

Coleman   Is it full of moaning, Valene? It is.

Valene   And nothing but moaning. (*Mimicking.*) 'Getting your hairstyle insulted is no just cause to go murdering someone, in fact it's the worst cause I did ever hear.'

Coleman (*laughing*)   That was a funny voice.

Girleen   I did order him this heart on a chain out of me mam's Freeman's catalogue. Only this morning it came. I asked him to be writing me with his new address last night, so I could send it on to him. I'd've never've got up the courage to be giving it him to his face. I'd've blushed the heart out of me. Four months I've been saving up to buy it him. All me poteen money. (*Crying.*) All me poteen money gone. I should've skittered it away the boys in Carraroe, and not go pinning me hopes on a feck I knew full well I'd never have.

Girleen *cuts the chain in two with the knife.*

Coleman   Don't be cutting your good chain there, Girleen.

Valene   Be leaving your chaineen there now, Girleen.
That chain looks worth something.

Girleen *tosses the chain in a corner.*

Girleen (*sniffling*)   Have you read the letter there, now?

Valene   I have. A pile of oul bull.

Girleen   I read it to see if he mentioned me. Not a word.

Coleman   Just shite is it, Valene? It's not worth reading?

Valene   Not at all.

Coleman   I'll leave it so, for I've no time for letters. I've
never seen the sense in them. They're just writing.

Girleen   I did like the bit about him betting his soul on ye.
Didn't ye like that bit?

Valene *picks up the broken chain.*

Valene   I don't think I understood that bit.

Girleen (*pause*)   Father Welsh drowned himself in the lake
last night, same place as Tom Hanlon. They dragged his
body out this morning. His soul in hell he's talking about,
that only ye can save for him. (*Pause.*) You notice he never
asked me to go saving his soul. I'd've liked to've saved his
soul. I'd've been honoured, but no. (*Crying.*) Only mad
drunken pig-shite feck-brained thicks he goes asking.

Shocked, **Coleman** *reads the letter.* **Girleen** *goes to the door.*
Valene *offers the pendant out to her.*

Valene   Your heart, Girleen, be keeping it for yourself.

Girleen (*crying*)   Feck me heart. Feck it to hell. Toss it into
fecking shite is the best place for that fecking heart.
(*Exiting.*) Not even a word to me!

After **Girleen** *exits,* **Valene** *sits in an armchair, looking at the
chain.* **Coleman** *finishes reading the letter, leaves it on the table and
sits in the opposite armchair.*

Valene   Did you read it?

Coleman   I did.

Valene (*pause*)   Isn't it sad about him?

Coleman   It *is* sad. Very sad.

Valene (*pause*)   Will we be trying for ourselves? To get along, now?

Coleman   We will.

Valene   There's no harm in trying.

Coleman   No harm at all, sure.

Valene (*pause*)   Poor Father Welsh Walsh Welsh.

Coleman   Welsh.

Valene   Welsh. (*Pause.*) I wonder why he did it?

Coleman   I suppose he must've been upset o'er something.

Valene   I suppose. (*Pause.*) This is a pricey chain. (*Pause.*) We'll be giving it back to her next time we see her. She's only shocked now.

Coleman   Aye. She's not in her right mind at all. She did hurt me hair when she tugged at it too, d'you know?

Valene   It did look like it hurt.

Coleman   It did hurt.

Valene (*pause*)   Father Welsh going topping himself does put arging o'er Taytos into perspective anyways.

Coleman   It does.

Valene   Eh?

Coleman   It does.

Valene   Aye. Awful perspective. Awful perspective.

Coleman (*pause*)   Did you see 'Roderick' his name is?

Valene (*snorts*)   I did.

Coleman (*pause. Seriously*)   We shouldn't laugh.

Valene *nods. Both pull serious faces. Blackout.*

Scene Seven

Room tidier. **Welsh**'s *letter pinned to the foot of the crucifix.* **Valene** *and* **Coleman** *enter dressed in black, having just attended* **Welsh**'s *funeral,* **Coleman** *carrying a small plastic bag full of sausage rolls and vol-au-vents. He sits at the table.* **Valene** *opens his poteen biscuit tin.*

Valene   That's that, then.

Coleman   That's that, aye. That's Father Welsh gone.

Valene   A good do.

Coleman   Aye. It's often a good do when it's a priest they're sticking away.

Coleman *empties his bag onto table.*

Valene   You didn't have to go nabbing a whole bagful, now, Coleman.

Coleman   Didn't they offer, sure?

Valene   But a whole bagful, I'm saying.

Coleman   It'd have only gone to waste, and sure a bagful won't be going very far between us.

Valene   Between us?

Coleman   Of course between us.

Valene   Ohh.

They both eat a little.

These are nice vol-au-vents.

Coleman   They *are* nice vol-au-vents.

Valene   You can't say the Catholic Church doesn't know how to make a nice vol-au-vent, now.

Coleman   It's their best feature. And their sausage rolls aren't bad either, although they probably only buy them in.

Valene (*pause*)   Em, would you be having a glass of poteen with me, Coleman?

Coleman (*shocked*)   I would, now. If you can spare a drop, like.

Valene   I can easy spare a drop.

Valene *pours two glasses, one bigger than the other, thinks about it, then gives* **Coleman** *the bigger.*

Coleman   Thank you, Valene. Sure we have our own little feasteen now.

Valene   We do.

Coleman   D'you remember when as gasurs we did used to put the blankets o'er the gap between our beds and hide under them like a tent it was o'er us, and go having a feasteen of oul jammy sandwiches then?

Valene   That was you and Mick Dowd used to go camping in the gap between our beds. You'd never let me be in with yous at all. Ye used to step on me head if I tried to climb into that camp with you. I still remember it.

Coleman   Mick Dowd, was it? I don't remember that at all, now. I did think it was you.

Valene   Half me childhood you spent stepping on me head, and for no reason. And d'you remember when you pinned me down and sat across me on me birthday and let the stringy spit dribble out your gob and let down and down it dribble 'til it landed in me eye then?

Coleman   I remember it well, Valene, and I'll tell you this. I did mean to suck that spit back up just before it got to your eye, but what happened I lost control o'er it.

Valene   And on me birthday.

Coleman (*pause*)   I do apologise for dribbling in your eye and I do apologise for stepping on your head, Valene. On Father Welsh's soul I apologise.

Valene   I do accept your apology so.

Coleman   Although plenty of times as a gasur I remember you dropping stones on me head while I was asleep and big stones.

Valene   Only in retaliation them stones ever was.

Coleman   Retaliation or not. Waking up to stones dropped on ya is awful frightening for a small child. And retaliation doesn't count anyways if it's a week later. It's only then and there retaliation does apply.

Valene   I do apologise for dropping stones on you so. (*Pause.*) For your brain never did recover from them injuries, did it, Coleman?

Coleman *stares at* **Valene** *a second, then smiles.* **Valene** *smiles also.*

Valene   This is a great oul game, this is, apologising. Father Welsh wasn't too far wrong.

Coleman   I hope Father Welsh isn't in hell at all. I hope he's in heaven.

Valene   *I* hope he's in heaven.

Coleman   Or purgatory at worst.

Valene   Although if he's in hell at least he'll have Tom Hanlon to speak to.

Coleman   So it won't be as if he doesn't know anybody.

Valene   Aye. And the fella off *Alias Smith and Jones*.

Coleman   Is the fella off *Alias Smith and Jones* in hell?

Valene   He is. Father Welsh was telling me.

Coleman   The blond one.

Valene   No, the other one.

Coleman   He was good, the other one.

Valene   He was the best one.

Coleman   It's always the best ones go to hell. Me, probably straight to heaven I'll go, even though I blew the

head off poor dad. So long as I go confessing to it anyways.
That's the good thing about being Catholic. You can shoot
your dad in the head and it doesn't even matter at all.

Valene   Well it matters a little bit.

Coleman   It matters a little bit but not a big bit.

Valene (*pause*)   Did you see Girleen crying her eyes out, the
funeral?

Coleman   I did.

Valene   Poor Girleen. And her mam two times has had to
drag her screaming from the lake at night, did you hear,
there where Father Walsh jumped, and her just standing
there, staring.

Coleman   She must've liked Father Welsh or something.

Valene   I suppose she must've. (*Taking out* **Girleen**'s
chain.) She wouldn't take her chaineen back at all. She
wouldn't hear tell of it. I'll put it up here with his letter to us.

*He attaches the chain to the cross, so the heart rests on the letter, which
he gently smoothes out.*

It's the mental they'll be putting Girleen in before long if she
carries on.

Coleman   Sure it's only a matter of time.

Valene   Isn't that sad?

Coleman   Awful sad. (*Pause. Shrugging.*) Ah well.

He eats another vol-au-vent. **Valene** *remembers something, fishes in
the pockets of his jacket, takes out two ceramic figurines, places them on
the shelf, uncaps his pen almost automatically, thinks better of marking
them as before, and puts the pen away.*

I think I'm getting to like vol-au-vents now. I think I'm
developing a taste for them. We ought to go to more funerals.

Valene   They do have them at weddings too.

Coleman   Do they? Who'll next be getting married round
here so? Girleen I would used to have said, as pretty as she is,

only she'll probably have topped herself before ever she gets married.

Valene   *Me* probably'll be the next one getting married, as handsome as I am. Did you see today all the young nuns eyeing me?

Coleman   Who'd go marrying you, sure? Even that no-lipped girl in Norway'd turn you down.

Valene (*pause. Angrily*)   See, I'm stepping back now . . . I'm stepping back, like Father Walsh said and I'm forgiving ya, insulting me.

Coleman (*sincerely*)   Oh . . . oh, I'm sorry now, Valene. I'm sorry. It just slipped out on me without thinking.

Valene   No harm done so, if only an accident it was.

Coleman   It *was* an accident. Although remember you did insult me there earlier, saying I was brain-damaged be stones as a gasur, and I didn't even pull you up on it.

Valene   I apologise for saying you was brain-damaged as a gasur so.

Coleman   No apology was necessary, Valene, and I have saved you the last vol-au-venteen on top of it.

Valene   You have that last vol-au-vent, Coleman. I'm not overly keen on vol-au-vents.

Coleman *nods in thanks and eats the vol-au-vent.*

Valene   Weren't them young nuns lovely today now, Coleman?

Coleman   They was lovely nuns.

Valene   They must've known Father Welsh from nun college or something.

Coleman   I'd like to touch them nuns both upstairs and downstairs, so I would. Except for the fat one on the end.

Valene   She was a horror and she knew.

Coleman   If dad was there today he'd've just gone screaming at them nuns.

Valene   Why *did* dad used to go screaming at nuns, Coleman?

Coleman   I don't have an idea at all why he used to scream at nuns. He must've had a bad experience with nuns as a child.

Valene   If you hadn't blown the brains out of dad we could ask him outright.

Coleman *stares at him sternly.*

Valene   No, I'm not saying anything, now. I'm calm, I've stepped back, and I'm saying this quietly and without any spite at all, but you know well that that wasn't right, Coleman, shooting dad in the head on us. In your heart anyways you know.

Coleman (*pause*)   I *do* know it wasn't right. Not only in me heart but in me head and in me everywhere. I was wrong for shooting dad. I was dead wrong. And I'm sorry for it.

Valene   And I'm sorry for sitting you down and making you sign your life away, Coleman. It was the only way at the time I could think of punishing ya. Well, I could've let you go to jail but I didn't want you going to jail and it wasn't out of miserliness that I stopped you going to jail. It was more out of I didn't want all on me own to be left here. I'd've missed ya. (*Pause.*) From this day on . . . from this day on, this house and everything in this house is half yours again, Coleman.

Touched, **Coleman** *offers his hand out and they shake, embarrassed. Pause.*

Is there any other confessions we have to get off our chests, now we're at it?

Coleman   There must be millions. (*Pause.*) Crushing your crisps to skitter, Valene, I'm sorry for.

Valene   I forgive you for it. (*Pause.*) Do you remember that holiday in Lettermullen as gasurs we had, and you left your

cowboy stagecoach out in the rain that night and next
morning it was gone and mam and dad said 'Oh it must've
been hijacked be Indians'. It wasn't hijacked be Indians. I'd
got up early and pegged it in the sea.

Coleman (*pause*)   I did love that cowboy stagecoach.

Valene   I know you did, and I'm sorry for it.

Coleman (*pause*)   That string of gob I dribbled on you on
your birthday. I didn't try to suck it back up at all. I wanted
it to hit your eye and I was glad. (*Pause.*) And I'm sorry for it.

Valene   Okay. (*Pause.*) Maureen Folan did once ask me to
ask you if you wanted to see a film at the Claddagh Palace
with her, and she'd've driven ye and paid for dinner too, and
from the tone of her voice it sounded like you'd've been on a
promise after, but I never passed the message onto ya, out of
nothing but pure spite.

Coleman   Sure that's no great loss, Valene. Maureen
Folan looks like a thin-lipped ghost, with the hairstyle of a
frightened red ape.

Valene   But on a promise you'd've been.

Coleman   On a promise or no. That was nothing at all to
go confessing. Okay, it's my go. I'm winning.

Valene   What d'you mean, you're winning?

Coleman (*thinking*)   Do you remember your Ker-Plunk
game?

Valene   I *do* remember me Ker-Plunk game.

Coleman   It wasn't Liam Hanlon stole all them marbles
out of your Ker-Plunk game at all, it was me.

Valene   What did you want me Ker-Plunk marbles for?

Coleman   I went slinging them at the swans in Galway. I
had a great time.

Valene   That ruined me Ker-Plunk. You can't play Ker-
Plunk without marbles. And, sure, that was *both* of ours Ker-

Plunk. That was just cutting off your nose to spite your face, Coleman.

Coleman   I know it was and I'm sorry, Valene. Your go now. (*Pause*.) You're too slow. D'you remember when we had them backward children staying for B & B, and they threw half your *Spiderman* comics in on the fire? They didn't. D'you know who did? I did. I only blamed them cos they were too daft to arg.

Valene   They was good *Spiderman* comics, Coleman. Spiderman went fighting Doctor Octopus in them comics.

Coleman   And I'm sorry for it. Your go. (*Pause*.) You're too slow . . .

Valene   Hey. . . !

Coleman   D'you remember when Pato Dooley beat the skitter out of you when he was twelve and you was twenty, and you never knew the reason why? I knew the reason why. I did tell him you'd called his dead mammy a hairy whore.

Valene   With a fecking chisel that Pato Dooley beat me up that day! Almost had me fecking eye out!

Coleman   I think Pato must've liked his mammy or something. (*Pause*.) I'm awful sorry for it, Valene.

Coleman *burps lazily.*

Valene   You do sound it!

Coleman   Shall I be having another go?

Valene   I did pour a cup of piss in a pint of lager you drank one time, Coleman. Aye, and d'you know what, now? You couldn't even tell the differ.

Coleman (*pause*)   When was this, now?

Valene   When you was seventeen, this was. D'you remember that month you were laid up in hospital with bacterial tonsilitis. Around then it was. (*Pause*.) And I'm sorry for it, Coleman.

Coleman   I do take your poteen out its box each week, drink the half of it and fill the rest back up with water. Ten years this has been going on. You haven't tasted full-strength poteen since nineteen eighty-fecking-three.

Valene (*drinks. Pause*)   But you're sorry for it.

Coleman   I suppose I'm sorry for it, aye. (*Mumbling.*) Making me go drinking piss, and not just anybody's piss but *your* fecking piss . . .

Valene(*angrily*)   But you're sorry for it, you're saying?!

Coleman   I'm sorry for it, aye! I'm fecking sorry for it! Haven't I said?!

Valene   That's okay, so, if you're sorry for it, although you don't sound fecking sorry for it.

Coleman   You can kiss me fecking arse so, Valene, if you don't . . . I'm taking a step back now, so I am. (*Pause.*) I'm sorry for watering your poteen down all these years, Valene. I am, now.

Valene   Good-oh. (*Pause.*) Is it your go now or is it mine?

Coleman   I think it might be your go, Valene.

Valene   Thank you, Coleman. D'you remember when Alison O'Hoolihan went sucking that pencil in the playground that time, and ye were to go dancing the next day, but somebody nudged that pencil and it got stuck in her tonsils on her, and be the time she got out of hospital she was engaged to the doctor who wrenched it out for her and wouldn't be giving you a fecking sniffeen. Do you remember, now?

Coleman   I do remember.

Valene   That was me nudged that pencil, and it wasn't an accident at all. Pure jealous I was.

Pause. **Coleman** *throws his sausage rolls in* **Valene**'s *face and dives over the table for his neck.* **Valene** *dodges the attack.*

And I'm sorry for it! I'm sorry for it! (*Pointing at letter.*) **Father Welsh! Father Welsh!**

Valene *fends* **Coleman** *off. They stand staring at each other,* **Coleman** *seething.*

Coleman   Eh?!!

Valene   Eh?

Coleman   I did fecking love Alison O'Hoolihan! We may've been married today if it hadn't been for that fecking pencil!

Valene   What was she doing sucking it the pointy end inwards anyways? She was looking for trouble!

Coleman   And she fecking found it with you! That pencil could've killed Alison O'Hoolihan!

Valene   And I'm sorry for it, I said. What are you doing pegging good sausage rolls at me? Them sausage rolls cost money. You were supposed to have taken a step back and went calming yourself, but you didn't, you just flew off the handle. Father Welsh's soul'll be roasting now because of you.

Coleman   Leave Father Welsh's soul out of it. This is about you sticking pencils down poor girls' gobs on them.

Valene   That pencil is water under a bridge and I've apologised whole-hearted for that pencil. (*Sits down.*) And she had boss-eyes anyways.

Coleman   She didn't have boss-eyes! She had nice eyes!

Valene   Well there was something funny about them.

Coleman   She had nice brown eyes.

Valene   Oh aye. (*Pause.*) Well it's your go now, Coleman. Try and top that one for yourself. Heh.

Coleman   Try and top that one, is it?

Valene   It is.

Coleman *thinks for a moment, smiles slightly, then sits back down.*

Coleman   I've taken a step back now.

Valene   I can see you've taken a step back.

Coleman   I'm pure calm now. It does be good to get things off your chest.

Valene   It *does* be good. I'm glad that pencil-nudging's off me chest. I can sleep nights now.

Coleman   Is it a relief to ya?

Valene   It *is* a relief to me. (*Pause.*) What have you got cooking up?

Coleman   I have one and I'm terrible sorry for it. Oh terrible sorry I am.

Valene   It won't be near as good as me pencilling poor boss-eyed Alison, whatever it is.

Coleman   Ah I suppose you're right, now. My one's only a weeny oul one. D'you remember you always thought it was Mairtin Hanlon snipped the ears off of poor Lassie, now?

Valene (*confidently*)   I don't believe you at all. You're only making it up now, see.

Coleman   It wasn't wee Mairtin at all. D'you know who it was, now?

Valene   Me arse was it you. You'll have to be doing better than that, now, Coleman.

Coleman   To the brookeen I dragged him, me scissors in hand, and him whimpering his fat gob off 'til the deed was done and he dropped down dead with not a fecking peep out of that whiny fecking dog.

Valene   D'you see, it doesn't hurt me at all when you go making up lies. You don't understand the rules, Coleman. It does have to be true, else it's just plain daft. You can't go claiming credit for snipping the ears off a dog when you didn't lay a finger on that dog's ears, and the fecking world knows.

Coleman (*pause*)   Is it evidence, so, you're after?

Valene   It *is* evidence I'm after, aye. Go bring me evidence
you did cut the ears off me dog. And be quick with that
evidence.

Coleman   I won't be quick at all. I will take me time.

He slowly gets up and ambles to his room, closing its door behind him.
Valene *waits patiently, giving a worried laugh. After a ten-second
pause,* **Coleman** *ambles back on, carrying a slightly wet brown paper
bag. He pauses at the table a moment for dramatic effect, slowly opens
the bag, pulls out a dog's big fluffy black ear, lays it on top of* **Valene**'s
head, takes out the second ear, pauses, places that on **Valene**'s *head
also, puts the empty bag down on the table, smoothes it out, then sits
down in the armchair left.* **Valene** *has been staring out into space all
the while, dumbstruck. He tilts his head so that the ears fall down onto
the table, and he stares at them a while.* **Coleman** *picks up* **Valene**'s
felt-tip pen, brings it over and lays it on the table.

Coleman   There's your little pen, now, Val. Why don't you
mark them dog's ears with your V, so we'll be remembering
who they belong to.

He sits back down in the armchair.

And do you want to hear something else, Valene? I'm sorry
for cutting off them dog's ears. With all me fecking heart I'm
sorry, oh aye, because I've tooken a step back now, look at
me . . .

He half-laughs through his nose. **Valene** *gets up, stares blankly at*
Coleman *a moment, goes to the cupboard right and, with his back to*
Coleman*, pulls the butcher's knife out of it. In the same brief second*
Coleman *stands, pulls the shotgun down from above the stove and sits
down with it.* **Valene** *turns, knife ready. The gun is pointed directly
at him.* **Valene** *wilts slightly, thinks about it a moment, regains his
courage and his anger, and slowly approaches* **Coleman***, raising the
knife.*

Coleman (*surprised, slightly scared*)   What are you doing,
now, Valene?

Valene (*blankly*)   Oh not a thing am I doing, Coleman,
other than killing ya.

Coleman   Be putting that knife back in that drawer, you.

Valene   No, I'll be putting it in the head of you, now.

Coleman   Don't you see me gun?

Valene   Me poor fecking Lassie, who never hurt a flea.

Valene *has gotten all the way up to* **Coleman**, *so that the barrel of the gun is touching his chest. He raises the knife to its highest point.*

Coleman   What are you doing, now? Stop it.

Valene   I'll stop it, all right . . .

Coleman   Father Welsh's soul, Valene. Father Wel . . .

Valene   Father Welsh's soul me fecking arse! Father Welsh's soul didn't come into play when you hacked me dog's ears off him and kept them in a bag!

Coleman   Ar that was a year ago. How does that apply?

Valene   Be saying goodbye to the world, you, ya feck!

Coleman   *You'll* have to be saying goodbye to the world too, so, because I'll be bringing you with me.

Valene   Do I look like I mind that at all, now?

Coleman (*pause*)   Er er, wait wait wait, now . . .

Valene   Wha . . . ?

Coleman   Look at me gun. Look at me gun where it's going, do ya see . . . ?

Coleman *slides the gun away and down from* **Valene**'s *chest 'til it points directly at the door of the stove.*

Valene (*pause*)   Be pointing that gun away from me stove, now.

Coleman   I won't be. Stab away, now. It's your stove it'll be'll be going with me instead of ya.

Valene   Leave . . . what . . . ? That was a three-hundred-pound stove now, Coleman . . .

Coleman   I know well it was.

Valene Be leaving it alone. That's just being sly, that is.

Coleman Be backing off you with that knife, you sissy-arse.

Valene (*tearfully*) You're not a man at all, pointing guns at stoves.

Coleman I don't care if I am or I'm not. Be backing off, I said.

Valene You're just a . . . you're just a . . .

Coleman Eh?

Valene Eh?

Coleman Eh?

Valene You're not a man at all, you.

Coleman Be backing away now, you, cry-baby. Be taking a step back for yourself. Eheh.

Valene (*pause*) I'm backing away now, so I am.

Coleman That'd be the best thing, aye.

Valene *slowly retreats, lays the knife on the table and sits down there sadly, gently stroking his dog's ears.* **Coleman** *is still pointing the gun at the stove door. He shakes his head slightly.*

Coleman I can't believe you raised a knife to me. No, I can't believe you raised a knife to your own brother.

Valene You raised a knife to me own dog and raised a gun to our own father, did a lot more damage than a fecking knife, now.

Coleman No, I can't believe it. I can't believe you raised a knife to me.

Valene Stop going on about raising a knife, and be pointing that gun away from me fecking stove, now, in case it does go off be accident.

Coleman Be accident, is it?

Valene Is the safety catch on that gun, now?

Coleman   The safety catch, is it?

Valene   Aye, the safety catch! The safety catch! Is it ten million times I have to be repeating meself?

Coleman   The safety catch, uh-huh . . .

He jumps to his feet, points the gun down at the stove and fires, blowing the right-hand side apart. **Valene** *falls to his knees in horror, his face in his hands.* **Coleman** *cocks the gun again and blows the left-hand side apart also, then nonchalantly sits back down.*

No, the safety catch isn't on at all, Valene. Would you believe it?

Pause. **Valene** *is still kneeling there, dumbstruck.*

And I'll tell you another thing . . .

He suddenly jumps up again and, holding the shotgun by the barrel, starts smashing it violently into the figurines, shattering them to pieces and sending them flying around the room until not a single one remains standing. **Valene** *screams throughout. After* **Coleman** *has finished he sits again, the gun across his lap.* **Valene** *is still kneeling. Pause.*

And don't go making out that you didn't deserve it, because we both know full well that you did.

Valene (*numbly*)   You've broken all me figurines, Coleman.

Coleman   I have. Did you see me?

Valene   And you've blown me stove to buggery.

Coleman   This is a great gun for blowing holes in things.

Valene (*standing*)   And now you do have no bullets left in that great gun.

He lazily picks the knife back up and approaches **Coleman**. *But as he does so* **Coleman** *opens the barrel of the gun, tosses away the spent cartridges, fishes in his pocket, comes out with a clenched fist that may or may not contain another cartridge, and loads, or pretends to load, the bullet into the gun, without* **Valene** *or the audience at any time knowing if there is a bullet or not.* **Coleman** *snaps the barrel shut and lazily points it at* **Valene***'s head.*

There was no bullet in that hand, Coleman! No bullet at all!

Coleman Maybe there wasn't, now. Maybe it's pretending I am. Be taking a pop for yourself.

Valene I *will* be taking a pop for meself.

Coleman And then we'll see.

Valene (*long pause*) I want to kill you, Coleman.

Coleman Ar, don't be saying that, now, Val.

Valene (*sadly*) It's true, Coleman. I want to kill you.

Coleman (*pause*) Try so.

Coleman *cocks the gun. Pause.* **Valene** *turns the knife around and around in his hand, staring at* **Coleman** *all the while, until his head finally droops and he returns the knife to the drawer.* **Coleman** *uncocks the gun, stands, and lays it down on the table, staying near it.* **Valene** *idles to the stove and touches the letter pinned above it.*

Valene Father Welsh is burning in hell, now, because of our fighting.

Coleman Well did we ask him to go betting his soul on us? No. And, sure, it's pure against the rules for priests to go betting anyways, neverminding with them kinds of stakes. Sure a fiver would've been overdoing it on us, let alone his soul. And what's wrong with fighting anyways? I do like a good fight. It does show you care, fighting does. That's what oul sissy Welsh doesn't understand. Don't you like a good fight?

Valene I *do* like a good fight, the same as that. Although I don't like having me dog murdered on me, and me fecking dad murdered on me.

Coleman And I'm sorry for your dog and dad, Valene. I *am* sorry. Truly I'm sorry. And nothing to do with Father Welsh's letter is this at all. From me own heart this is. The same goes for your stove and your poor figurines too. Look at them. That was pure temper, that was. Although, admit it, you asked for that stove and them figurines.

Valene You never fecking stop, you. (*Pause.*) *Are* you sorry, Coleman?

Coleman I am, Valene.

Valene (*pause*) Maybe Father Walsh's Welsh's soul'll be all right so.

Coleman Maybe it will, now. Maybe it will.

Valene He wasn't such a bad fella.

Coleman He wasn't.

Valene He wasn't a great fella, but he wasn't a bad fella.

Coleman Aye. (*Pause.*) He was a *middling* fella.

Valene He was a *middling* fella.

Coleman (*pause*) I'm going out for a drink for meself. Will you be coming with me?

Valene Aye, in a minute now I'll come.

Coleman *goes to the front door.* **Valene** *looks over the smashed figurines sadly.*

Coleman I'll help you be clearing your figurines up when I get back, Valene. Maybe we can glue some of them together. Do you still have your superglue?

Valene I do have me superglue, although I think the top's gone hard.

Coleman Aye, that's the trouble with superglue.

Valene Ah, the house insurance'll cover me figurines anyways. As well as me stove.

Coleman Oh . . .

Valene (*pause*) What, 'oh'?

Valene Do you remember a couple of weeks ago there when you asked me did I go stealing your insurance money and I said no, I paid it in for you?

Valene I do remember.

Coleman (*pause*)   I didn't pay it in at all. I pocketed the lot of it, pissed it up a wall.

Valene, *seething, darts for the gun.* **Coleman** *dashes out through the front door.* **Valene** *brings the gun to the door and chases out, but* **Coleman** *is long gone.* **Valene** *returns a few seconds later, gun in hand, shaking with rage, almost in tears. After a while he begins to calm down, taking deep breaths. He looks down at the gun in his hands a moment, then gently opens the barrel to see if* **Coleman** *had really loaded it earlier. He had.* **Valene** *takes the cartridge out.*

Valene   He'd've fecking shot me too. He'd've shot his own fecking brother! On top of his dad! On top of me stove!

He tosses the gun and cartridge away, rips **Father Welsh**'s *letter off the cross, knocking* **Girleen**'s *chain onto the floor, brings the letter back to the table and takes out a box of matches.*

And you, you whiny fecking priest. Do I need your soul hovering o'er me the rest of me fecking life? How could anybody be getting on with that feck?

He strikes a match and lights the letter, which he glances over as he holds up. After a couple of seconds, the letter barely singed, **Valene** *blows the flames out and looks at it on the table, sighing.*

(*Quietly.*) I'm too fecking kind-hearted is my fecking trouble.

He returns to the cross and pins the chain and letter back onto it, smoothing the letter out, and letting the chain swing in front of it like a pendulum. He puts on his jacket, checks it for loose change and goes to the front door.

Well I won't be buying the fecker a pint anyways. I'll tell you that for nothing, Father Welsh Walsh Welsh.

Valene *glances back at the letter a second, sadly, looks down at the floor, then exits. Lights fade, with one light lingering on the crucifix and letter a half second longer than the others.*

Methuen Drama Contemporary Dramatists

include

John Arden (two volumes)
Arden & D'Arcy
Peter Barnes (three volumes)
Sebastian Barry
Dermot Bolger
Edward Bond (eight volumes)
Howard Brenton
  (two volumes)
Richard Cameron
Jim Cartwright
Caryl Churchill (two volumes)
Sarah Daniels (two volumes)
Nick Darke
David Edgar (three volumes)
David Eldridge
Ben Elton
Dario Fo (two volumes)
Michael Frayn (three volumes)
John Godber (three volumes)
Paul Godfrey
David Greig
John Guare
Lee Hall (two volumes)
Peter Handke
Jonathan Harvey
  (two volumes)
Declan Hughes
Terry Johnson (three volumes)
Sarah Kane
Barrie Keefe
Bernard-Marie Koltès
  (two volumes)
Franz Xaver Kroetz
David Lan
Bryony Lavery
Deborah Levy
Doug Lucie

David Mamet (four volumes)
Martin McDonagh
Duncan McLean
Anthony Minghella
  (two volumes)
Tom Murphy (five volumes)
Phyllis Nagy
Anthony Neilson
Philip Osment
Gary Owen
Louise Page
Stewart Parker (two volumes)
Joe Penhall
Stephen Poliakoff
  (three volumes)
David Rabe
Mark Ravenhill
Christina Reid
Philip Ridley
Willy Russell
Eric-Emmanuel Schmitt
Ntozake Shange
Sam Shepard (two volumes)
Wole Soyinka (two volumes)
Simon Stephens
Shelagh Stephenson
David Storey (three volumes)
Sue Townsend
Judy Upton
Michel Vinaver
  (two volumes)
Arnold Wesker (two volumes)
Michael Wilcox
Roy Williams (two volumes)
Snoo Wilson (two volumes)
David Wood (two volumes)
Victoria Wood

Methuen Drama World Classics

include

Jean Anouilh (two volumes)
Brendan Behan
Aphra Behn
Bertolt Brecht (eight volumes)
Büchner
Bulgakov
Calderón
Čapek
Anton Chekhov
Noël Coward (eight volumes)
Feydeau
Eduardo De Filippo
Max Frisch
John Galsworthy
Gogol
Gorky (two volumes)
Harley Granville Barker
  (two volumes)
Victor Hugo
Henrik Ibsen (six volumes)
Jarry

Lorca (three volumes)
Marivaux
Mustapha Matura
David Mercer (two volumes)
Arthur Miller (five volumes)
Molière
Musset
Peter Nichols (two volumes)
Joe Orton
A. W. Pinero
Luigi Pirandello
Terence Rattigan
  (two volumes)
W. Somerset Maugham
  (two volumes)
August Strindberg
  (three volumes)
J. M. Synge
Ramón del Valle-Inclán
Frank Wedekind
Oscar Wilde

Methuen Drama Modern Plays

include work by

Edward Albee
Jean Anouilh
John Arden
Margaretta D'Arcy
Peter Barnes
Sebastian Barry
Brendan Behan
Dermot Bolger
Edward Bond
Bertolt Brecht
Howard Brenton
Anthony Burgess
Simon Burke
Jim Cartwright
Caryl Churchill
Complicite
Noël Coward
Lucinda Coxon
Sarah Daniels
Nick Darke
Nick Dear
Shelagh Delaney
David Edgar
David Eldridge
Dario Fo
Michael Frayn
John Godber
Paul Godfrey
David Greig
John Guare
Peter Handke
David Harrower
Jonathan Harvey
Iain Heggie
Declan Hughes
Terry Johnson
Sarah Kane
Charlotte Keatley
Barrie Keeffe

Howard Korder
Robert Lepage
Doug Lucie
Martin McDonagh
John McGrath
Terrence McNally
David Mamet
Patrick Marber
Arthur Miller
Mtwa, Ngema & Simon
Tom Murphy
Phyllis Nagy
Peter Nichols
Sean O'Brien
Joseph O'Connor
Joe Orton
Louise Page
Joe Penhall
Luigi Pirandello
Stephen Poliakoff
Franca Rame
Mark Ravenhill
Philip Ridley
Reginald Rose
Willy Russell
Jean-Paul Sartre
Sam Shepard
Wole Soyinka
Simon Stephens
Shelagh Stephenson
Peter Straughan
C. P. Taylor
Theatre Workshop
Sue Townsend
Judy Upton
Timberlake Wertenbaker
Roy Williams
Snoo Wilson
Victoria Wood

For a complete catalogue of Methuen Drama titles
write to:

Methuen Drama
36 Soho Square
London
W1D 3QY

or you can visit our website at:

www.methuendrama.com